'One of the most thought-provoking boc [...] come across. Heather Hansen's vast m [...] to differences, corporate politics savvy, and pra[...] *Unmuted* a "must read" business book in 2022.'

Laurie Schloff, Executive Communication Coach and author of bestselling book Smart Speaking: 60 Second Strategies for More than 100 Speaking Problems and Fears

'I have always felt that connection and contribution are at the heart of good leadership, and you can't achieve either without strong communication skills. *Unmuted* will give you the courage to speak up in the world, and to do so in a conscious and connected way. This book is an essential guide for authentic leaders at every level who want to make a difference in their organization and inspire others to do the same.'

Jiak See Ng, Deloitte Asia Pacific Financial Advisory Leader

'Finally, a holistic and realistic framework for today's communication challenges.'

Kyle D. Hegarty, author of The Accidental Business Nomad

'In hospitals today, communication is essential for patient safety and team cohesion. This book gives you the tools to clearly convey your ideas when it matters most, while remaining true to your identity and background.'

Juan B Grau, MD, FACC, FACS, Full Professor of Surgery, Director of Cardiothoracic Surgical Services, The Valley Hospital Health Care System in alliance with The Cleveland Clinic Foundation, The University of Ottawa Heart Institute

'If you're interested in improving your communication skills, *Unmuted* is a must read. Heather approaches communication differently than most, with a focus on self-awareness and cultural sensitivity. This book is nothing like any communication book you've ever read, and one you'll refer to again and again.'

Heather Hansen, award-winning attorney and author of the Amazon bestseller The Elegant Warrior

'As the world changes, so does the way we communicate. *Unmuted* is a communication guide for our modern, digital age – a refreshing read that couldn't have come at a better time. I have benefitted tremendously from the lessons in this book and will use it as a reference moving forward. This is required reading for anyone who aspires to be a more confident communicator.'

James Lim, Executive Vice President and President, Greater Asia
BD (Becton, Dickinson and Company)

'Getting along with people who think and behave differently is extremely hard until we can get along with ourselves. The more confident, conscious and connected we are, the less we can be muted, especially when our voice is needed the most. *Unmuted* is the blueprint to make it happen.'

Csaba Toth, author of Uncommon Sense in Unusual Times

'Heather Hansen delivers a cutting-edge solution combining communicative competence, language, linguistic and cultural awareness. Her warmth and skill as a trainer and learning and development consultant give us the push we need to get re-engaged with the new world around us more directly, positively and confidently. *Unmuted* is a must-read for leaders big and small focused on Diversity, Equity and Inclusion.'

Bettina Anagnostopoulos, Language and Communication
Solutions Leader, Cartus Corporation

HEATHER HANSEN

UNMUTED

HOW TO SHOW UP, SPEAK UP AND INSPIRE ACTION

B L O O M S B U R Y   B U S I N E S S
LONDON • OXFORD • NEW YORK • NEW DELHI • SYDNEY

BLOOMSBURY BUSINESS
Bloomsbury Publishing Plc
50 Bedford Square, London, WC1B 3DP, UK
29 Earlsfort Terrace, Dublin 2, Ireland

First published in Great Britain 2022

A catalogue record for this book is available from the British Library

Library of Congress Cataloguing-in-Publication data has been applied for

ISBN: 978-1-4729-9380-9; eBook: 978-1-4729-9381-6

2 4 6 8 10 9 7 5 3 1

Typeset by Deanta Global Publishing Services, Chennai, India
Printed and bound in Great Britain by CPI Group (UK) Ltd, Croydon CR0 4YY

To find out more about our authors and books visit www.bloomsbury.com and sign up
for our newsletters

For my husband, Peter,
who never allows me to press mute
(even if he sometimes secretly wishes I would).

And for our daughters, Victoria and Stella.
Stay forever unmuted.

Scan this QR code or visit www.heatherhansen.com/unmuted to access
additional resources including your **Unmuted Assessment, Unmuted
Discussion Guides** for each chapter and the **Unmuted Action Guide**
to help you transform your organization into an unmuted workplace.

Contents

 Introduction

'You're on mute!'

After hearing and saying this phrase for the millionth time, it finally struck me that many of us really are on mute. Not just in the confines of virtual meetings and breakout rooms, but in our lives, our careers and even in our families.

Lost in the digital, artificially intelligent, VUCA world[1] of the Fourth Industrial Revolution, we are often overwhelmed and paralyzed by the complexity of modern life. With serious threats to our planet, our health and our livelihoods, the easiest escape is to press mute and silence our voices. But this isn't a virtual meeting. Pressing mute on our lives is the worst thing we can do in a complex world that demands our participation.

The world has changed, and to succeed we can't stay quiet. We need to grow and adapt. Remote work, global teams, hybrid offices and work from home structures are changing the professional landscape and presenting us with new challenges. How can we communicate with and relate to people we'll probably never meet in person? How can we build trust in a world dominated by social media and artificial intelligence, where it's harder to distinguish what's real from what's fake?

We're desperate to trust and believe in each other and our leaders again, but the only way to conquer challenges the world has never seen is with ideas the world has never heard. We need new voices, new perspectives and new leadership.

We need *you* – unmuted.

Whether you're at the beginning of your career or 30 years in, this book will help you become a more conscious, confident and connected communicator. It offers practical strategies for conquering the world's newest challenges. You'll learn to develop yourself and your team so that every voice is heard and the best ideas shine.

What will it take for you to show up, speak up and inspire action in the world, in your organization or even in your family and friendships? Can the world afford *not* to hear your voice?

Maybe you're fighting impostor syndrome and think your ideas aren't good enough. Perhaps you've tried to share your ideas, but they've always fallen on deaf ears. Or maybe you've yelled so loudly for so long that no one wants to listen anymore.

My hope is that, as you read this book, it will help you to identify what is holding you back, and how you might unmute yourself to make the greatest impact in your life, your work and your community. In turn, I hope you'll be inspired to unmute others by creating environments where open and honest communication thrives, diversity and inclusion are the norm, and innovation flourishes.

✶✶✶

In early 2020, as most of the world went into lockdown during the COVID-19 pandemic, we watched every aspect of our lives change at a pace we've never experienced before.

Seemingly overnight, we went from being collective societies to isolated family units or individuals. Travel was banned; borders were closed. The only things keeping us connected were the Internet and virtual communication tools.

Managers were at a loss trying to figure out how to navigate these changes. When I asked a group of top leaders in a global logistics firm to describe how they were feeling at work, 123 of them (based everywhere from Europe to Australia) expressed this shared human condition with words like 'busy', 'challenged', 'stressed' and 'exhausted'.

The focus of leaders across every industry turned almost entirely to their people. How could they get their teams to connect, communicate and collaborate from a distance? These weren't new challenges for globally dispersed teams, but the pandemic seemed to act like a magnifying glass. Problems that existed before came into sharper focus, and solving these problems became more urgent.

This isn't a book about COVID-19, yet the pandemic made the importance of human connection and understanding more prominent. Once we could see into each other's living rooms, vulnerability in the workplace became more acceptable. In an age of robotics and digitalization, our leaders and teams seemed more human, and we were reminded of what really mattered – our relationships.

However, many leaders were still confused. Ironically, they didn't know what it meant to be human. How did they need to show up? What should they say? How could they positively impact the organization, keep morale high and foster this feeling of connection not only now but moving forward? One leader asked me in desperation, 'What are your other clients like me doing right now?'

That's when I realized it was time for me to unmute and write this book.

✶✶✶

I certainly don't have all the answers. Over the last 15 years in my role as a consultant, trainer and coach, I have had the unique opportunity to be a detached observer.

I'm in the fortunate position where I get to have private conversations with top leaders in global companies and hear first-hand their struggles, dreams and bright ideas. I also see what is holding them back. How they express themselves to me in a safe and confidential coaching environment is quite different from how they face their peers, their clients, other stakeholders and the world.

On the other side of the equation, when I run training programmes for their teams, I hear complaints about these same leaders and the company culture. I hear when team members feel held back and why they are disengaged. When new ideas are met with 'But, my boss won't like that', we usually have a problem.

Whether the problem is a lack of innovation and ideation, poor team efficiency and collaboration or low levels of engagement and inclusion, we can trace most challenges back to the way people communicate (or don't).

It's from these observations, conversations and experiences that the Unmuted Framework has emerged. Although communication might seem like a linear activity in which a message is sent from person A to person B, the reality is much more complicated. Communication is influenced by who A and B are, their understanding of themselves and each other, their communicative competencies, their relationship to each other and their shared environment.

Take it from me, a frustrated learning and development practitioner, training is only one small part of the solution, and it is usually only treating the symptoms. You can throw as much presentation skills training at your people as you'd like. It doesn't mean they'll suddenly come up with better ideas to present or be more willing to share their ideas in a toxic environment. We need to look at the whole puzzle, not just the individual pieces.

This is what the Unmuted Framework attempts to do. It takes a more holistic view of global business communication. It pulls from organizational psychology, cultural studies and linguistics to give a full picture of how we can communicate to build trust and collaboration in our organizations. Even more, I hope it will encourage you to go one step further and inspire action in our world.

✷✷✷

As I set about writing this book, I knew that I wanted to integrate additional learning elements that could help you dig deeper into the content. My goal was to make it a more interactive experience with videos and handouts that you could use for self-reflection or in discussions with your team. Visit www.heatherhansen.com/unmuted or scan the QR code, which you'll find at the front and back of the book, to gain access to the Unmuted Resources.

Start with the Unmuted Assessment. This assessment will place you along the three axes of the Unmuted Framework to determine where your strengths and weaknesses lie and on which parts of the book you should focus your attention.

As you work through the book, be sure to pause at the end of each chapter to access the Unmuted Discussion Guide for that chapter. Watch the video and take notes on your journal handout (pdf file) as you reflect on how you can apply the concepts of this book to your life. The Unmuted Discussion Guides are powerful tools for self-reflection, and are extremely helpful to drive conversation if you are reading *Unmuted* with your team or in a book club.

The book itself is broken into four parts. The first three relate to each section of the Unmuted Framework: conscious, confident and connected communication. Part IV then puts everything together to show you how to unmute yourself and your organization. Before we dig into each section, the next chapter describes the Unmuted Framework in detail. You'll learn how conscious, confident and connected communication coincide to enable an unmuted communication culture where everyone thrives. You'll also see how missing one of the elements can lead to negative consequences for the individual and the organization. This explanation of the Unmuted Framework is required reading for the rest of the book.

You can confidently jump between the first three parts of the book to focus on the area(s) where you need help the most. Each part will dig deeper into that area of the framework, the research that supports it and the specific strategies you can apply to improve performance. I hope that curious readers will refer to the endnotes and look up the interesting articles, studies and books that have contributed to shaping my ideas. Each chapter can stand alone, but you'll get the greatest understanding from reading all the chapters in each part together.

Part I of this book focuses on conscious communication and how to show up in the world.

In order to understand and connect with others, we first need to understand ourselves, our perceptions of others and how others perceive us. We all need to be more self-aware. This section will help to untangle the ideas of consciousness and self-awareness so that we can take actionable steps towards greater understanding.

We start with our thoughts and how we define ourselves – our identities. We look at the science behind how our brains work to form unconscious biases. You'll be forced to question who you are, what you value and why. You'll also see why embracing difference is imperative for your success.

Much of this book looks at communication through a global lens, but I'll argue that all our interpersonal relationships are intercultural. Even if you have never left your hometown, you need to be able to not just understand others but also adapt your behaviours to them. This takes cultural intelligence. Learning to authentically adapt and present your best self will help you to connect with people who are different from you. We'll also question whether authenticity and adaptation can coexist and how adaptation differs from manipulation.

A discussion of conscious communication would not be complete without analyzing the role of the listener and how we can listen better. We love to focus on the speaker as the driving force of successful (or unsuccessful) communication, but the listener's abilities carry equal, if not greater, weight.

Finally, we'll look at how the way your organization communicates contributes to (or detracts from) your diversity and inclusion agenda. We'll discuss how to address microinequities and how we can break through our unconscious biases to give all ideas equal weight.

In Part II, we turn to confident communication and how to speak up and share your great ideas.

Do you have the language and communication skills to speak up with confidence in the world? This section will shatter many of the common beliefs we have around the language of global business and the skills that are necessary to speak with confidence. We'll look at the link between confidence and competence in a world that is filled with very confident but not always competent leaders.

From the psychology of speaking anxiety to a redefinition of 'bad' English, this section will reprioritize the skills that are needed to unmute in our modern, global world. Whether English is your only language or your fifth language, it's important to understand how this global language is changing. You will learn how to listen and speak in ways that invite greater participation so you can better understand and are always understood.

We will also look at how to adapt our old face-to-face communication skills to become more confident virtual communicators. We need to make some important changes to our body language and tone and learn to connect through technology.

Part III shifts our focus to the third area of the framework: connected communication.

If you want to inspire others to take action and are concerned with creating a dynamic company culture that supports inclusion, innovation and collaboration, this final section will be the most important one for you.

This section focuses on our relationships in the workplace, why they are so important and how we can create psychologically safe environments where unmuted communication thrives. We'll see why relationships are the key to happiness (and longevity) and how we can create stronger relationships at work.

We'll enter the world of people analytics to uncover how modern technology and big data can help us understand the way our teams connect and communicate, and when and why they don't. You'll learn how you can draw a data-driven map of your organization to see exactly where communication and connection are breaking down. You'll also be able to identify the influencers in your organization and find out how best to align with them.

The success of our organizations hinges on unmuted leadership in a psychologically safe environment. We'll discuss how to decrease social distance while increasing psychological safety in your team. These concepts are even more important for dispersed teams who are communicating through the new rules of netiquette in the digital age.

Once you have a deep understanding of the elements that make up unmuted communication, Part IV will show you how to apply them in your own life and in your organization. If you are ready to transform your team, business unit, or entire organization, scan the Unmuted Resources QR code to access the Unmuted Action Guide. This guide explains how to get started implementing the many lessons you'll learn in this book.

All the chapters are designed to be quick reads that give you something new to think about. Dip in and out of the book according to your needs in the moment, but keep in mind the importance of a strong foundation in all three areas. To be truly unmuted in your communication and relationships, a good balance of conscious, confident and connected communication is key.

I hope this book and the Unmuted Framework will inspire you to show up and speak up about the issues that are important to you and the changes you want to see in the world. In turn, I hope you inspire the same action in others. We need your voice, your ideas and your leadership.

It's time to unmute.

🎙 The Unmuted Framework

What does it mean to be unmuted? When you are unmuted you know how to voice your ideas with confidence, without fear of judgement, in a way that is well-received by others. You inspire others to do the same by also knowing when it's time to mute and be an encouraging, listening ear.

Many people have difficulty sharing their ideas clearly and confidently. They usually think there is a skills gap: 'I need better ___ skills' (fill in the blank: speaking, language, pronunciation, assertiveness).

This is the easy answer, and you can buy books full of tips on delivering the perfect presentation, speaking assertively, designing better slides, managing difficult conversations and so on. You probably have some of them on your bookshelf. I know I do.

Taking this skills approach, however, oversimplifies the situation. I could teach you everything I know about delivering a perfect presentation. If you don't have the self-confidence to deliver it, the self-awareness to read your audience and know how they are reading you or if you're delivering it in a toxic environment, you won't succeed, no matter how great your skills are.

The Unmuted Framework takes a more holistic approach to communication. In addition to speaking skills and communicative *confidence*, it also looks at how *conscious* you are in your communication and how *connected* you are with those in your environment. Only when all three elements are present, can you truly be unmuted.

Let's take a closer look at each of these elements to see how they come together to create an unmuted culture where everyone's ideas are heard and appreciated.

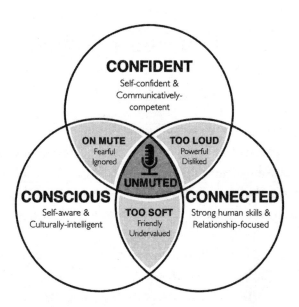

Conscious communication

Awareness is at the heart of human connection. It builds trust and enhances empathy.

In this framework, conscious communication refers to how you show up in the world. What are your values and beliefs, how do they differ from the people around you and how do they cause you to behave (and communicate) in certain ways?

The gurus say, 'Just be authentic!' but many people don't know who they are or what they stand for. How can you be authentic if you don't know what your values are or where you got them (hint: they were given to you).

You can only understand others, and find the best way to connect with them, when you first understand yourself. This takes a degree of cultural intelligence and sensitivity mixed with strong social skills. By cultural intelligence, I do not mean 'big C' national culture stereotypes but all the smaller cultural filters that have defined you from birth. These filters change the way you see and experience the world. We'll take a much closer look at these in Chapter 2.

Do you know your blind spots and why you have them? When you meet someone for the first time and click in the first 30 seconds, what is it that is so appealing? Often even more important, what is it about someone that makes you have a 'bad feeling' and not want to trust them?

Many of us are familiar with making these judgements, but we rarely know why. It actually has to do with the way our brains function. The conscious communicator knows how their brain works for good and bad, creating assumptions that could backfire on them. They know how to slow their thinking to identify microinequities and speak in a way that is more inclusive. Many of the habits that we developed as humans to enhance our survival can come in the way of making rational judgements and weighing the ideas of different people equally.

Another element of knowing yourself is to understand how others perceive you. Do *you* give *them* that 'bad feeling' when you meet them? Or do most people find you appealing? How can you adapt the way you show up in the world so that you present your best self?

When you understand yourself, your values and how people normally perceive you, it's easier to adjust your behaviour to suit your situation and context. Your awareness determines the language you choose, the tone of your voice and the strength of your message.

Lacking self-awareness, it is hard to read a situation and understand others. Those who do not have cultural intelligence or know how to authentically adapt to different situations present their ideas in a way that does not resonate or create an impact. These people are often misunderstood and disliked. Neither reaction helps to advance one's message (or career).

Confident communication

The next part of our framework deals with your confidence. Do you believe in your ideas, and do you have the language and communication skills to express them? Are you so focused on being perfect – finding the right words, using proper grammar, sharing the right story – that your perfection paralysis is forcing you to turn down your volume?

Confidence in your *skills* is an easy problem to solve through coaching and training. We'll cover many of these communication skills in Part II of this book. What is much harder is to instil confidence in your *self*. If you don't believe in yourself or your ideas, suffer from impostor syndrome or think you don't deserve to be in the position you've worked hard to reach, then all the skills courses will do nothing for you. You'll need to dig deeper to find answers to why you feel this way.

It's very natural to feel self-conscious when we want to share our ideas with the world. Every one of my clients asks me whether their presentation is good enough; do they look alright, is that story as funny as they think, does it all make sense? The importance of your message far outweighs the risk involved with delivering it.

I smile because, as I type this, I'm also reminding myself to live my own mantra and stay unmuted – to share my ideas without fear of judgement – and we've barely even started. Will you judge me and this book? Of course. Can I control your reactions? Not really. Sharing the Unmuted message and inspiring the right people who resonate with it is more important to me than trying to control or foresee the feedback and reception that I will receive. I need to be willing to take that risk.

In the discussion about confidence in Part II, you'll learn ways to gain the self-confidence and the skills confidence to fully express yourself. You'll discover what's really keeping you from speaking up and how to overcome it.

Connected communication

Obviously, when we are unmuted, we aren't speaking into the void. We are part of a community, whether that be a workplace, a home, a social group or a larger public sphere. You can have all the confidence and awareness in the world, but if your environment does not support open communication, your thoughts and feelings will fall on deaf ears. Worse, your ideas will fall on hostile ears that judge and demean you when you share your message.

This challenge is one that people think is out of their control and it is the largest missing piece in organizations: an inclusive and psychologically safe environment built on strong human relationships.

Our teams can only be open and honest and come up with brilliant new ideas when there is no fear of failure, ridicule or judgement. You can't expect people to show up to your meeting with cameras on and headsets ready if they feel like their presence isn't valued. They also won't risk speaking up to share their great ideas if they are worried that you'll respond negatively and embarrass them in front of the group.

Connected communicators know the importance of their relationships and develop strong interpersonal skills. They are aware of their environment and the relational dynamics in it. They measure engagement and connection on a regular basis to make improvements to their systems, just as they would with any other performance indicator. And now, as we are deeply entrenched in the digital age and are faced with a wider variety of remote work options, connected communicators know how to choose their communication channels appropriately.

Why these elements matter

It's only when we are conscious, confident *and* connected that we can live an unmuted life, have an unmuted career and become an unmuted leader. An improper balance leads to you being too loud, too soft or fully on mute. Let's look at what happens in situations where we are missing one of these three fundamental elements.

Confident and Connected, but not Conscious = TOO LOUD

If people are fully confident and are operating in a safe, connected environment, but they have no self-awareness or cultural intelligence, they likely dominate discussions and easily offend others. In the worst case, they interrupt, force their opinions, compete instead of collaborate and speak to be heard, even when they have little to say.

They come on too strong. Their voices are just too loud. They project a powerful persona but have little impact because people have stopped listening. In the worst cases, they are seen as offensive, arrogant and self-centred with no sense of appropriateness or social grace.

It's rare we meet people who are this extreme, though they certainly do exist. Often, people who lack awareness don't mean to be rude or dominant. They just don't see how their behaviour affects others.

Conscious and Connected, but not Confident = TOO SOFT

You could have a company with an amazing, connected culture full of self-aware and culturally sensitive people who still don't have the confidence to speak up. Perhaps they are worried about their English or think their ideas aren't good enough. Maybe there is a cultural difference that keeps them from being more outspoken within the group. Or, maybe they are just more introverted. They are very aware, and they know their comments would be welcome, but still can't seem to speak up.

These people turn down their volume. If they aren't nudged by others to speak up and take part, they blend into the background and disappear. It doesn't mean these people are disengaged. They could be actively listening and diligently doing their work.

Still, they are overlooked and undervalued. They just aren't seen. In our rapidly advancing world, where technology is developing at the speed of light, if you fall into this category, you could soon be out of work. The only way to stand out in our digital world run on artificial intelligence is through your human contribution. If you don't have the confidence to speak up and contribute, people will begin to question what your contribution is.

One pattern that has been seen in high-performing teams is that their members have equal talk time. Everyone shares their ideas and participates actively. This has nothing to do with forcing an introvert to speak up. Even introverts are happy to contribute when they are part of a conscious, psychologically safe community.

If you are lacking confidence in either yourself or your skill set and have turned down your volume, people may overlook and undervalue your contribution to the team.

Confident and Conscious, but not Connected = ON MUTE

Finally, what happens when members of your team are confident and aware, but they are operating in a toxic environment where they don't feel safe to share their ideas? In short, they become fearful, get frustrated and press that mute button.

They might try to express themselves, knowing they have good ideas. After being rejected, embarrassed or ignored enough times, they finally just stop talking. There are too many negative repercussions to speaking up, and regardless, no one cares what they say anyway.

This is the worst loss of human potential we can have in an organization. When our best people, who have bright ideas and lots of social awareness, disengage, they often take others with them. Through their frustration, they will eventually leave the organization and go to a competitor who values their input.

Balancing the unmuted organization

As leaders in an organization, your job is to balance the three areas of the framework. Of course, you need to lead by example and unmute yourself first. When people see you take risks to communicate openly, show vulnerability and have empathy, they will follow. When they trust that it's okay to make mistakes and there are no bad ideas, they'll be more willing to contribute.

It's also your job to balance the personalities in your environment – turn down the voices that are too loud, turn up the quiet ones and encourage a healthy, connected culture where no one stays on mute.

When you have all the ideas on the table, instead of just the loudest ones, and all the ideas are considered with the same rigour, imagine what your team will be able to achieve!

🎙 PART I: SHOW UP

Conscious Communication

🎙 Who are you?

'None of you are normal. You are all cultural outliers.
If you weren't, you wouldn't be here.'[1]

As university students attending our first anthropology class, we looked around the room at each other wondering how our professor, Dr Barb West, could say such a thing. We couldn't *all* be outliers, could we? Maybe the guy sitting next to me was, but surely not *me*. Is she saying I'm not normal? This was not the message my young adult ego needed when I so desperately wanted to fit in on my new university campus. It was already declared: I didn't belong.

As Barb went on to explain, almost all of us in that class had chosen majors within the School of International Studies. If we truly fit into our own culture and thought we could find everything we could ever want or need within it, we wouldn't take an interest in international relations. We certainly wouldn't have chosen a school that required study abroad.

I left the United States (with the intention that the move would be permanent) just one month after graduation. I've spent the last 20 years living abroad on two continents. I think it's safe to say that Barb was right.

This is one of only a few college lectures that I still remember with full clarity. It spurred my first existential crisis and demonstrated precisely why we go to university in the West: to figure out who we are and what our individual contribution to the world will be. Most of us make it to graduation without ever figuring this out. In fact, we go most of our lives without knowing who we are. A quick Google search of 'Who am I?' returns 19.48 billion results.[2]

How can we show up in the world if we don't even know who we are, what we stand for, and how we can contribute? How can you begin to unmute when you have no idea what you're here to say?

This is where we begin, with a not so simple question: Who are you?

If I asked you to tell me your life story, you'd probably land on a few important memories, perhaps some that are similar to my college lecture. You'd start 'connecting the dots'[3] to show me how your past perfectly led to your present and where you will likely go in the future. You'd tell me about teachers, coaches or mentors who made a strong impression on you. You'd tell me your stories of struggle and triumph, experiences that have shaped your view of the world, and turning points that made you who you are today.

Why do you think these stories stand out in your mind? Which stories, experiences and people are you forgetting? What about the stories and experiences that didn't make sense – that don't seem to directly relate to where you are today?

How do *you* change if you choose different stories? Or, how do you change if you create a different meaning from the stories you have chosen to tell?

In 2001, Dan McAdam, a professor in the Department of Psychology at Northwestern University, defined these stories as your 'narrative identity',[4] which can and does change over time as you collect more experiences and continue to make sense of who you are. The stories you choose to tell, and the meaning you make of them, can have a very significant impact on your feelings of fulfilment and on other positive mental health markers.

One study found that people who have multiple stories of triumph over personal struggle, for example, have a stronger commitment to making an impact on society and helping others.[5]

That research, however, was carried out in the US, where the cultural narrative of the 'American Dream' is all about overcoming hardship and finding success despite difficult circumstances. Every

American is raised with an awareness of this narrative. Consciously or unconsciously, it will have some influence on the stories they tell about their life journey.

This cultural aspect of identity cannot be overlooked. Phillip Hammack, a cultural psychologist at University of California, Santa Cruz, refers to cultural influences as a 'master narrative'.[6] He explains that we design our narrative identities within the constructs of our cultural norms and our historic place in time.

You might be familiar with the phrase, 'The winners write history.' This is a good example of how master narratives form.

I was confronted with one of my master narratives the first time I visited the War Remnants Museum in Ho Chi Minh City (Saigon). Originally named the Exhibition House for US and Puppet Crimes, you can imagine how different the story of their 'American War' was to the narrative of the 'Vietnam War' that I was taught in school, heard from my parents (who lost many friends there) and saw repeated in the media growing up. It's important to have your master narratives challenged and to see the world in different ways.

How you respond to these challenges is up to you. Some people get angry and reject alternative narratives. This is a good sign that a strongly-held master narrative is being challenged. Some people manage to move beyond anger to see the world through different eyes. Recognize the differences (you don't have to agree with them) and identify how your master narrative has contributed to your values and beliefs.

This is where we begin to find our authentic selves, identify the values that are important to us and organize our life lessons in the filing cabinets of our minds.

As you start to recognize how your culture has shaped you, you'll start to realize that you didn't consciously choose many of your beliefs. They were given to you by parents, teachers, your favourite films, and society at large. Have you ever stopped to question your beliefs? If you didn't choose them, then who are you, really? Maybe it's time to reinvent yourself!

Your changing identity

When we only draw on our past experiences to try to define our present and future, we can easily get stuck. As soon as we need to grow, or try something new, or stretch outside of our comfort zone, the sudden growing pains of impostor syndrome creep in.

'Who am I to act like this? This isn't me. My story hasn't prepared me for this.' But why not? We are all changing and growing, and our story needs to grow with us.

Herminia Ibarra turns the identity narrative on its head in her book *Act Like a Leader, Think Like a Leader*.[7] She argues that you can only grow into a new role and begin to think like a leader after you have started to act like one. You need to start *doing* before you can develop your story and identity around a new role. Your past stories can't prepare you for future roles you have yet to step into.

Ibarra recommends a three-step process for how we can transition into new roles or develop ourselves to step out of our comfort zone. She refers to this as the 'outright principle' where you need to work from the outside in, and not the inside out:

1) Dive into new activities, roles and responsibilities (change your actions).
2) Surround yourself with new people and experiences (change your network).
3) Redefine yourself (change your thinking).

By following this process, you write new stories, discover new sides of yourself and gain confidence in new behaviours and skills.

It's a bit like moving to a new country. You need to adapt. Nothing in your past has prepared you for how you'll need to behave to be successful in your new culture. You just need to dive in and start participating. You take part in new activities. You start building a new network and learning from others – many others, not just one or two. You aren't imitating any one person in particular, but you are choosing your responses carefully. You change your behaviours, communication styles and maybe even your posture and tone of voice in ways you think might work for you. You try them out. You experiment. And as you determine what works best and what you feel most comfortable with, you start to redefine yourself. You alter your story. Your identity changes. You must act first before your new way of thinking follows.

You don't need to move to a different country to expand your comfort zone and see your identity change. You probably had an almost identical experience the last time you got a new job and joined a new company. When you take on a new role with new responsibilities, and you want to get it right, you can plan on there being a serious learning curve and a significant change to how you define yourself.

Developing a growth mindset

This process of trial and error and figuring things out requires a positive attitude towards learning. As we'll see in Part III, a growth (or learning) mentality is not only important for you as you begin to press unmute more in your life and career; it's also important for your team, organization or family to embrace a culture of learning.

If you want to grow, you need to be ready to make mistakes. Our fear of failure can be paralyzing. If you never take risks, you won't get the rewards. Being vulnerable and compassionate towards yourself and others when mistakes are made (because there will be mistakes) is all part of growing.

Brené Brown is known the world over for her work on vulnerability. When talking about a learning culture, she explains the difference between the 'knower', who is concerned with always *being* right, versus the 'learner', who is working towards *getting* things right.[8] This requires a degree of vulnerability to be able to say that you don't always have the answers and you are learning too.

Putting all of this through the lens of culture, you can imagine that these ideas will be more difficult to embrace and, in some cases, will be rejected outright by different cultures in the world. Many people believe that apologizing for a situation is the same as taking responsibility and admitting fault. Asking for help or not having the answer shows a lack of competence. Sharing your struggles is showing weakness. Yet, in these same cultures, you will see an urgency to learn, improve and grow – almost an obsession with outperforming.

It may not be easy, but we know that country culture is not the same as a company's culture or the actual preferences of the individual. Through conscious hiring decisions and the creation of a strong company culture of honesty, transparency and a growth mindset, it is possible (with some effort) to create unmuted cultures at work. We'll take a closer look at culture, perception and identity in Chapter 2.

Finding *you*

It takes bravery, and also vulnerability, to face the world without fear and unmute. Vulnerability is an often-misunderstood concept. It does not mean having to be super emotional at work, crying with your colleagues or sharing the intimate details of your personal life.

Brené Brown defines vulnerability as, 'daring to show up and let ourselves be seen'.[9] In the unmuted framework, our focus is not only to be seen, but also heard, acknowledged and understood. It's about being honest and transparent while bringing your best self to all areas of your life. It's speaking up when you believe that something is important and knowing that you have an important message to share. It's putting your ideas out into the world, acknowledging that you'll likely receive feedback and criticism. When you do receive criticism, it's about being confident and self-aware enough to consider it before deciding whether you will accept or reject it. Vulnerability also means having the humility to empower others to do the same.

When it comes to your identity, the only constant is change. You might know who you are today, but tomorrow you can choose to define yourself in a completely different way. A more important question as you strive to press unmute in your life is, 'Who do you want to become?'

Press UNMUTE

- Self-reflection is important to identify your identity narrative and the stories that define you, but you also need to be prepared to change your stories, create new meaning from them, choose new stories or create ones from scratch.
- Dive in and take action, and learn as you go. Surround yourself with new people and opportunities to grow.
- Approach situations with curiosity and a growth mindset that allows you to experiment, fail, succeed and learn. Focus on 'getting it right' instead of 'being right'.
- Get comfortable being vulnerable and showing more of your true self. If you lead the way, others will follow.

2

🎤 The power of perception

'Do you know how to handle this car? This is a man's car, you know...'[1]

The sweet salesgirl tries not to react to her customer's comment. She smiles and slips behind the wheel. Little does the customer know, she is Leona Chin, a professional motorsport athlete. Five seconds later, she has him screaming like a baby as she takes him on the ride of his life.

This prank was organized by Mitsubishi Motors in Malaysia in collaboration with Maxmen TV, a company that creates viral videos with pranks and social experiments. It was almost too easy to pull this one off.

Who would guess that a small, young, gorgeous woman with long, nicely curled hair could be a professional driver? A more important question is: Why wouldn't we guess that?

Our perceptions are powerful, and they are extremely difficult to change.

Right now, as you read this book, the words on the page are not the only things your brain is processing. Your awareness is greater than you can possibly imagine. Without thinking about it, your mind is processing everything in your surroundings – your comfort (or discomfort) in your chair, the clouds passing over the sun and the slight change in light this creates, a small chill from a draught or the warmth of the steam off your cup of tea. While you were reading these last few lines, you might have noticed your mind shifting focus to your surroundings, noticing the similarities and differences to the world I have created for you on the page. All this happens without your control. You aren't making conscious choices to do this.

If you are listening to this book, you are hearing these words, but you might also be wondering where my accent is from and how old I am. You've already decided how easy it will be for you to listen to me for another few hours. From the sound of my voice, you've filed away assumptions about me that match the reservoirs of data your subconscious mind has collected over the course of your unique life.

I can't possibly list all the pieces of information you are taking in right now, because research suggests our senses send 11 million bits of information to our brains every second. Our conscious mind can only process about 50 of them.[2] What is happening to the other 10,999,950 bits?

Daniel Kahneman, in his bestselling book *Thinking, Fast and Slow*, describes the brain as having two systems.[3] System 1, the 'fast-thinking brain' works without us knowing it. It pulls in those 10,999,950 bits of information, categorizes them, recognizes patterns and makes immediate judgements and choices, before you even realize what has happened.

This is where your perceptions are formed – instantaneous judgements about the world around you and the people in it, based on your unique personal history. Everything you have seen, heard, tasted, smelled, without even consciously knowing it, can be retrieved in an instant by the fast-thinking brain.

When you see another person for the first time, your fast-thinking brain goes to work. Based on characteristics as simple as the shape of their face and the degree of their smile, you've already decided on the person's trustworthiness and competence. One research study found that this happened in as quickly as one tenth of a second.[4] Your fast-thinking brain works hard, racing through catalogues of information stored outside the reach of your conscious thoughts.

System 2, Kahneman explains, is your slow-thinking brain. This part of the brain is capable of rational, conscious thought. It processes the 50 most important bits and makes logical, rational conclusions. This is the part of your brain that stops and says, 'Let's not judge too quickly...' But it's too late. The fast-thinking brain is already guilty of doing just that, and it will take time and effort on the part of your slow-thinking brain to rationally convince yourself otherwise.

Unconscious barriers

Children as young as three years old can identify 'nice' and 'strong' traits just by looking at pictures of faces.[5] We are *very* good at finding patterns, forming stereotypes and making assumptions. Kahneman says this is because our brains are, by nature, lazy.

We try to use the least amount of energy possible to find the easiest solutions. This is true of any challenge we might face in life. By creating patterns and having a mental filing cabinet of experiences, we can make more educated split decisions based on what we have seen in the past. This amazing capability is what allows us to perceive threats, and it has kept us safe for thousands of years.

But we have far fewer threats to our personal survival today and our worlds are much larger than the tribes our species began in. When we need to interact with people much different to ourselves, our fast-thinking brain sabotages us by misjudging new experiences and falling back on lazy stereotypes developed from our past.

Imagine you are studying astrophysics at university. Your favourite class is taught by a Nobel Prize winner who discovered a black hole at the centre of our Milky Way. Now, look carefully... What does your professor look like? Make a quick list of features.

What did you see? When I ask participants this question in my workshops, I receive many answers, but these three characteristics are always mentioned:

- Male
- Over 55 years old
- Glasses

Now, what if I told you this professor is Dr Andrea Ghez? A woman who turned 55 the same year she accepted the Nobel Prize in Physics in 2020, for work she started at the age of 30.

Although this is beginning to change, it's not surprising that the great majority of people would immediately see a man as our Nobel Prize-winning physics professor. Dr Ghez is only the fourth woman ever to win the award. Our brains overwhelmingly think of men as leaders in the sciences since women are under-represented in these fields.

It's completely understandable that our brains would jump to conclusions like this. The problem, however, is that this is how stereotypes are formed. This is why we have white privilege and we've never seen a female US President. Our brains are playing tricks on us. They are setting up unconscious, bias-filled barriers, and we aren't even aware that it is happening.

They are blind spots.

Blind spots and culture

It's actually a bit ironic to call these stereotypes blind spots because you can see the results of our blind spots all around us. They are hidden in plain sight within our cultures, our families, communities and countries. We just can't see them because they are camouflaged as 'normal' and 'common sense'.

When you travel outside your own community – it doesn't even need to be that far – you'll start to realize how uncommon 'common sense' really is. It's probably most obvious when you travel to another country and people look different, speak a different language and have obviously different systems and ways of doing things.

But let's look closer to home. What about joining a new company, moving to a different city or starting a new hobby? There could be new terminology and slang to deal with. There might be new group dynamics and politics to figure out. You might have people ask you where you are from or just instinctively know that you must be new because you don't quite belong.

It's easy to think that we're all ruled by logic and are in control of our decisions, but the reality is, we're ruled by the fast-thinking brain. Herein lies the dilemma.

Our brains, although having the best intentions, are working against us. They are reinforcing our own cultural norms, stereotypes and biases in every moment of our existence, and we have no control over it. How do we stop something that is happening unconsciously?

The first step is to make our slow-thinking brain aware of this process so it can begin to first see, and then question, the conclusions of the fast-thinking brain. We need to raise our self-awareness by consciously approaching and analyzing our subconscious.

This shouldn't come as a novel piece of advice. If you work for a larger company, you have probably done your fair share of personality profiles and 360-degree feedback reports. Self-development and leadership development starts with self-awareness. Once you understand your own beliefs, values and motivations, you can better understand and communicate with others.

How profiles can hurt and help

In our natural quest to understand ourselves and others, a multitude of personality assessments and profiles have been developed. All these profiles attempt to give some insight into our natural preferences and tendencies so that we can understand our own and others' behaviours better. Profiles can be helpful in hiring decisions, creating high-functioning teams and testing our fast-thinking brain's assumptions.

The problem with many of these profiles is that they tell you the *what* about yourself (for example, whether you are extrovert or introvert, thinking or feeling), but they don't tell you the *why* (your underlying values and beliefs that have shaped your fast-thinking brain).

Cultural assessments, on the other hand, focus more on the range of behaviours that are considered normal in a particular country but ignore the specific personality markers of the individual. The national lines of countries are incredibly misleading.

I can't tell you how many people have approached me in different countries and said, 'You're nothing like a "normal" American!' I laugh and wonder what a 'normal' American looks like to them. What is their perception of who I 'should' be or how I 'should' act? Depending on where I am in the world, those perceptions can be very different. In some places I hear the opposite, that I'm 'too American' with my big smile and melodic voice. I just shrug my shoulders.

Whether others see me as 'not American enough' or 'too American' says a lot more about their own perception of Americans and of me than who I actually am. No one is the perfect average of their typical national traits.

This leads me to one of the most important fundamentals of this book: *interpersonal relationships are intercultural relationships.*

Csaba Toth wrote about this connection between intercultural relationships and interpersonal relationships in his book *Uncommon Sense in Unusual Times.* He quotes research carried out by Taras, Steel and Kirkman which found that 80 per cent of the differences we see *across* country borders we can find *within* our individual countries.[6] We could have more values and beliefs in common with someone on the other side of the world than someone across the street. Studying culture according to variables such as profession, economic class and environmental characteristics could provide more meaning than country lines.

This means that a fashion designer in New York will probably share more cultural values with another fashion designer in Tokyo than they will with a construction worker doing renovation work in the office next door.

Why can't we approach our colleague in another department with the same care and curiosity as we would approach a colleague in another country? Just because we come from different parts of the world doesn't mean we are that different. Just because we live down the street from each other doesn't mean we are the same.

Toth demonstrates this point in his Wheel of Culture (see below), where he shows how every individual belongs to 10–20 different microcultural groups at a time, and that each of these influences the way we view the world.[7] Remember, your life experiences are feeding the fast-thinking brain and creating connections and patterns in your world view. Your unique filter could be influenced by any of the factors in the diagram.

The Wheel of Culture[8]

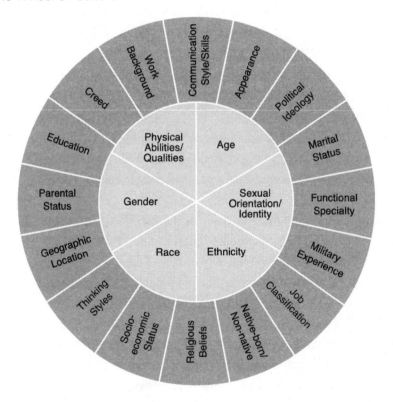

In my work and travels, I have certainly found that national background has little influence on how I relate and interact with others when we have enough of these cultural filters in common. When I work with teams within the Unmuted Framework, finding commonalities within this wheel prove more useful than finding differences.

Recognizing the need to combine personality traits with cultural drivers, Toth created the Global DISC profile. This assessment is the first to combine personality traits, such as those found in typical varieties of DISC assessments, with the cultural variations that explain underlying values. As he explains, the Global DISC looks at three levels of identity: the *what*, *how* and *why* we think, feel and behave so differently.[9]

Dealing with 'difficult' people

When you become more self-aware and begin learning about others and the differences between you, you will start to realize that 'difficult' people are just 'different' people. They see the world through different filters, have had different life experiences and their fast-thinking brains connect information and categorize it differently. Imagine what they must think about you!

Still, you might argue that some people are beyond acceptance. They have a reputation for being difficult. But why do you believe they are difficult? Probably because they prioritize their values differently than you do.

I have one client who I find very difficult. She is direct and curt in her messages. She always seems irritated and short on time. She can be demanding. I came to realize over time that she highly values time, detail, accuracy and efficiency. What I perceive as irritation and anger is actually just her focus on getting the job done. What's interesting is that I value all the same things, but I value people more. She is incredibly task-based, whereas I tend to be more focused on relationships.

I get annoyed with what I see as her lack of empathy. She gets annoyed with my small talk and sugar-coating. I still don't enjoy communicating with her, but instead of taking her behaviours personally, I can understand she is simply behaving according to her values. Once I understood this, it was much easier to work with her without going on the defensive and getting angry during our interactions. I could accept her for who she is as a person instead of judge her according to what I consider (through my filters) to be bad behaviour.

I value my relationship with her because she brings diversity to the table. If you can enter your relationships with curiosity and wonder, and can override your natural tendency to judge, imagine what you could achieve in your team.

It sounds like I'm looking through some rose-coloured glasses, I know. Of course, we sometimes must deal with people who don't hold our values at all. These people are difficult in a very different way, and it may go beyond your capability to understand and tolerate their behaviour. Here I am talking about racist or misogynistic colleagues or bosses, people who do not have integrity and take unethical or illegal actions or people that in some way violate your core beliefs and values. I would in no way endorse that you chalk up prejudice or abuse as 'bad behaviour'.

Press UNMUTE

- Start questioning your beliefs and assumptions. Is there a different way to look at a situation or person than your first impression?
- Slow down your thinking.
- Be curious about others and ask them how they see the world around them.
- Consider the many different filters you have in your life and how your behaviour changes depending on who you are with and the commonalities you share.

3

🎤 Authentic adaptability

'Who are *you*?' said the Caterpillar.
'I – I hardly know, sir, just at present – at least I know who I *was* when
I got up this morning, but I think I must have been changed several
times since then.'
Alice in Lewis Carroll's *Alice's Adventures in Wonderland*[1]

Do you ever feel like Alice?

Now that we can interact with people from every corner of the world, all in the same day and all from the comfort of home, we might change the way we show up in the world multiple times each day. Different languages, cultures and time zones all contribute to a whirl of identity shifts.

Even if you aren't working across cultures and borders, you probably deal with many different groups of people every day: family, friends, colleagues, bosses, clients … the list goes on. You go from being a loving parent to a guiding boss to a caring friend within hours – sometimes within minutes. You adapt your behaviours to each situation to give others what they need and have your needs met in return.

How can we both adapt to a situation and still remain authentic? Are we not being inauthentic when we try to fit in with a new group of people, whether it's a new social group, the parent association at your child's school or your colleagues in a foreign country?

The need for authentic leaders in our world today is strong, especially when trust in government, business and the media is lower than ever before.[2] We know the important roles that authenticity and vulnerability play in developing trust. But we often forget the importance of adaptability in how we express ourselves, especially to those who are different from us.

Being true to yourself

In Chapter 1 we looked at narrative identities and the way we use stories from our lives to support the beliefs we have about ourselves. In order to grow, develop and transition into new roles, we need to put ourselves in new situations, meet new people and create new stories about who we can be. We are constantly adapting and finding ways to make sense of the world around us.

Flipping between various roles and responsibilities and trying to connect in very different relationships can be exhausting. Authenticity *should* be the key to lightening this burden. The argument goes that if we are being our authentic selves in each of these roles, it shouldn't be difficult. We only feel drained when we are 'putting on a show' or trying to please others instead of being true to ourselves.

Bill George, a senior fellow at Harvard Business School, encourages us to integrate our lives in his book *True North*.[3] He uses the metaphor of a house to explain this concept of integration. If you had the parts of your life – personal, professional, family, friends – all separated into different rooms in your home, could you knock down the walls and still be the same person? If you can, he says, then you have integrated your life and are being truly authentic in your relationships.

But what if those walls are there for a reason? Our identities ebb and flow, and we choose to show different parts of ourselves depending on who we are with and the context of our situation. Our self-awareness, combined with our understanding of others and the context, drives decisions about how we show up and interact. It would be silly to think that anyone would behave the way they do during movie night with their kids while in a boardroom discussing business strategy with the CEO.

Does this mean that you are changing who you are or being inauthentic? Absolutely not.

Authenticity refers to *who we are*: our values and beliefs.

Adaptability refers to *how we express ourselves*: our actions and behaviours.

What's really needed is bringing your *best* self to a situation depending on the relationship and context, and acknowledging that it doesn't always have to be your *full* self. In fact, in most cases it won't be. And that's okay.

This is what I call 'authentic adaptability', and it might just be the single most important human skill for success in a constantly changing global world. It is also key to being a conscious communicator.

When adapting is inauthentic

Adapting goes too far when you begin compromising on your values in order to impress or gain acceptance from others. If you behave in a way that goes against your beliefs, then you have crossed the line into inauthenticity.

Many people inappropriately use 'authenticity' as an excuse for not meeting others halfway. 'Why should I have to change who I am for them?' There are very few cases where you are asked to change who you are. Authentic adaptation refers to consciously adjusting your behaviour (without compromising your values) in order to create a stronger connection and more understanding with others.

Here are three situations where you might (knowingly or unknowingly) adapt in an inauthentic way.

You don't know who you are

The biggest problem with the quest for authenticity is that most people have no idea who they are. If I asked you right now, 'What are your values?' could you name three right away? Have you given thought to who you are and what you stand for? Have you learned about the cultural influences you were raised with and identified your blind spots? If not, go back and review Chapters 1 and 2.

When we aren't fully self-aware, it is very easy to adapt without thinking things through. We change our behaviours without questioning whether our new behaviours align with our values and beliefs. In this case, we are simply being whoever others want us to be. This isn't what authentic adaptability is all about.

I challenge you to take some time to think about your values. What are the non-negotiable beliefs you carry that define who you are and how you show up in the world?

You knowingly behave in ways that go against your beliefs, values or physical safety

When you do know who you are but feel a need to behave in a way that directly contradicts your beliefs, you've crossed the line into inauthentic adaptation. Usually people are forced into this situation by some kind of authority – a company or a country – and do not choose this form of adaptation themselves.

When I first moved to Denmark, I joined a women's water polo team. I never would have thought that to play I'd be forced to inauthentically adapt. Scandinavian cultures are much more accepting of nudity than my puritanical American upbringing, and the Danes are not fans of the huge amounts of chlorine that we pour into our pools.

The combination of these factors has led to a regimented changing-room culture. You are required to undress fully in the changing room and enter an open, group shower. There are signs on the walls showing the specific body parts that should be washed with soap. The first time I was there, I entered the shower with my bathing suit on (as I typically would in the US if I was asked to shower before entering a pool, but even those rules are lax in California). A changing-room guard approached me and told me I had to take my bathing suit off and wildly pointed at the pictures on the signs. Then she proceeded to stand there watching me, to ensure I washed everywhere I should.

It was a shocking experience for me. I had been swimming competitively since age six and had never been forced to shower naked in front of a group of strangers, even if they were all the same sex. I hadn't even been naked in front of my family since I was very young.

I was forced to adapt if I wanted to play water polo, but this behaviour crossed a serious line for me. I was raised to believe that *my body is my own and no one can force me to show it without my permission.* This belief trumped all other ways I could have interpreted the situation.

The Danes have a very different interpretation. They tell me that our bodies are not something to be ashamed of and that it is totally normal (and more hygienic) to shower this way. In fact, when they were young (in late primary and early secondary school), the boys and girls would even shower together. No big deal!

There is no right or wrong. There are only cultural norms. When you are faced with a situation that forces you out of your comfort zone, only you can choose where you draw the line. Your values are yours to decide. But sometimes you'll find yourself in a culture (national, corporate, social or familial) that may not leave you any choice. Luckily for me, times have changed and you'll now find private shower stalls in public changing rooms in Denmark. Now I can participate and keep my dignity!

This might sound like an extreme (and off-topic) example, but how different is it from passing laws that require women to remove their hijabs at work? What if there is a strong anti-LGBTQ culture in the workplace, misogynistic and sexually abusive leaders, or constant microaggressions committed against different races? When we view inauthentic adaptation for what it is – peer pressure backed by an authority figure – it's easy to see why people leave non-inclusive companies. It's hard to contribute in a positive way if you feel truly inauthentic at work.

Your intentions are not pure

I'm often asked whether adaptation isn't just a code word for manipulation, but this is only the case if a person has bad intentions. If you are pretending to be someone you are not in order to get something that you need, then this is inauthentic at best, corrupt at worst. The great majority of people do not have bad intentions and are adapting because they truly want to create a connection. They want to make others feel comfortable.

Spotting inauthenticity

Luckily, we have inbuilt human sensors that go off when we are faced with inauthenticity. Have you ever met someone that just seemed 'off'? You probably had an uneasy feeling about them but didn't really know why. We typically feel this way when someone is being incongruent. Congruency refers to a person's words, tones and behaviour (body language) all being in sync with their mental and emotional state. When someone is incongruent, we get the feeling that they are hiding something, don't mean what they say or are being manipulative.

Sometimes people play with congruency. Sarcasm is a great example of purposeful incongruence. If you want to say something sarcastically, your words say one thing, but your tone and probably your body language say another. Think of the many ways you could say phrases like, 'Yeah, right...' or 'No way...' We play with congruency all the time.

Inauthenticity, on the other hand, becomes visible when a person doesn't realize they are not in sync. Maybe their words and tone sound confident but their eyes are darting around nervously. Or maybe someone is trying to act warm during a virtual meeting and they keep forcing a smile at odd places.

Often these incongruences arise when people feel insecure. The darting eyes show nervousness. The forced smile comes from awkwardness speaking into a camera and wanting to show friendliness. They are not necessarily trying to be something they are not. They just don't have the confidence yet to fully step into the role they are trying on at the moment. They are in the process of creating a new story, of developing, and just aren't quite there yet.

The exact opposite situation can also be true when a person is misread due to cultural differences. One of my clients, who is next in line for a role as CFO for Asia and Pacific (APAC) is very confident in her ideas, but her Western colleagues think she isn't. They think her overall demeanour and lack of eye contact signal weakness and a lack of confidence. As she confided in me, making eye contact doesn't come naturally to her, and it's not so important in her culture. Instead of working on growing confidence in her ideas, she is finding ways to hold eye contact with more confidence. It will take quite a bit of practice before she can do this in congruency and without it feeling (and looking) awkward.

As you can see, it takes an enormous level of self-awareness and understanding to read a situation appropriately and prevent our automatic sensors from making judgements.

How to adapt authentically

Authentic adaptability is a skill we can all develop, and we can start by increasing our cultural intelligence. Cultural intelligence is usually reserved for speaking about different national cultures, but as we discussed in Chapter 2, most of our interactions, even in our own cities and towns, can be considered intercultural. We all have different filters and ways of seeing the world. By increasing our cultural intelligence, we can understand everyone better, not just those from other countries.

Cultural intelligence is defined as being able to function and manage effectively in culturally diverse settings. We can look at cultural intelligence as using a combination of the brain, heart and body to better adapt to our circumstances.

Using the brain

There are two ways we can improve our cultural intelligence by using our brains. First, we need to think about cultural difference. This is a metacognitive process in which you increase your own awareness of how you process culture. You find your blindspots. Examine your own preferences as compared to others. Find the cultural differences and then adapt to them. Most importantly, approach every situation with an open, non-judgemental mind.

This metacognitive process happens from the moment you enter a room. Stop, watch and listen before you speak or act. Take in your surroundings. Feel the energy of the room. Watch for cultural markers that signal respect or the importance of hierarchy. Listen to how people speak and watch how people react to them. Is it okay to be direct, or do you need to listen between the lines? How do people sit, stand or move? Most importantly, what is different from how you would typically act, and how can you adjust and adapt to present yourself in a way that will be well received? The metacognitive process requires you to take a bird's-eye view of your surroundings. You need to be self-aware, aware of others and aware of their impressions of and reactions to you. Then you adjust accordingly.

The second brainy way to improve your adaptation skills is to learn more about the other culture or person. Having a greater understanding of the specific cultural norms among a group of people (whether it's your kid's football team or the Board of Directors) will help you know how to adapt and behave appropriately.

Basically, do your homework. If you're in a foreign country, learn about the cultural norms there, keeping in mind that you could meet individuals that don't fit all those norms. Even in your hometown, find out who you are meeting, what their interests are, how formal they tend to be, what the culture of their company is like. Interpersonal relationships should be approached with the same level of awareness as intercultural ones.

Using the heart

You must *want* to adapt to others and meet them halfway. Your motivation for adapting will be the strongest factor in whether you are able to successfully do so. Many people just don't want to change or step out of their comfort zones. They will often use 'authenticity' as their excuse, saying they need to be true to themselves and everyone else should just accept their behaviour.

Authentic adaptation allows you to be authentic to your core beliefs while also being motivated to connect with others in new ways. Approach people with a curious mind, an open heart and full respect for the unique talents they bring to the table. You can create meaningful relationships and achieve greater understanding. But you need to *want* it.

Using the body

The obvious step in adaptation is changing your physical behaviours. Use a different communication style than you are accustomed to. Experiment with a new leadership style. Try on some new roles and write some new stories. As we talked about in Chapter 2, if you start acting differently, you will start thinking differently, and what once was foreign can become your new normal.

Cultural intelligence, when applied correctly using the brain, heart and body, not only helps you to adapt to individual situations, but also helps you to adjust quickly to all kinds of change. Becoming more adaptable is an important leadership skill in our constantly developing world. Flexing your adaptation muscles prepares you to be more agile and resilient during times of crisis and transformation.

Press UNMUTE

- Know yourself. What do you stand for? What are your values? Where are the lines that you won't cross?
- Don't use 'authenticity' as your excuse for not adapting to others. You can change behavioural styles without changing who you are as a person.
- Align your words, tone and body language so that people feel you are being congruent. This isn't always easy when you are trying to adapt your style to new surroundings.
- Don't judge others too quickly for being inauthentic. Ironically, they might be trying to create a more authentic connection with you by trying something new.
- Think, feel and act in authentically adaptive ways so you can present your best self and meet others halfway.

4

🎙 Conscious listening

'What would the world be like if we were speaking powerfully to people who were listening consciously in environments which were actually fit for purpose?'[1]

This line is taken from Julian Treasure's Top 10 TED Talk 'How to Speak so That People Want to Listen'. It's been viewed almost 50 million times. The popularity of this message is a testament to our common need to feel heard and the equally common disappointment of being misunderstood or ignored.

We often place blame on the speaker when communication fails, as if communication only goes one way. He's too hard to understand? Fix his accent. She's too boring? Teach her storytelling skills. His English isn't good enough? Send him to lessons. She never speaks up? She must not have anything interesting to say.

What if we turn all of this around for a second? What if the listeners learned how to tune their ears to foreign accents? What if they listened with curiosity so that no topic is boring? What if they looked past the grammatical errors to listen to the message? What if they learned to be more supportive so people felt more confident?

In short – what if we learn how to listen so that people want to speak? By being as conscious about how we *listen* as how we *speak*, my hope is that we can achieve greater understanding as well as create more collaborative environments where people feel comfortable to unmute.

Remember, creating an unmuted culture is not about just pressing unmute whenever you like. It's just as important to know when to stay muted and listen. This is key to understanding different perspectives and giving equal consideration to everyone's ideas. We must slow down our fast-thinking brains to break through our biases to really hear, listen and understand.

Our discussion on conscious listening includes more than just hearing someone's words in a conversation taking place in real time. In this chapter, we'll look at all receptive behaviours where we are trying to make sense of a message. It could be creating meaning from an email, listening to a voice note or participating through a chat box. The way we process information, react and respond to messages is all included in our discussion here.

Taking turns and talk time

When looking at the factors that define a high-functioning team, one group of researchers found that the key was equal amounts of talk time by each member of the group.[2] Groups that took turns sharing their ideas and pulled on the strength of each member in equal measure ended up doing the best on a series of cognitive tests. This supported the hypothesis that teams could develop a kind of 'collective intelligence' that was greater than the sum of its parts.

We'll take a closer look at this study and related work in the field of psychological safety in Part III of this book. At this point, it's important to note that we must not only speak and share our ideas equally, but also listen equally. It's only when we all listen to each other that we can get the very best out of our groups. This takes conscious effort.

Communicating that you are listening

The way we speak, listen and take turns is all very cultural. An American friend married to a Swede said that his wife's family couldn't stand him when they met him. He never stopped talking. His discomfort with silence was in direct opposition to their enjoyment of it. Long pauses between speakers and breaks in conversations during meetings are a sign of deep thinking and thoughtful discussion. For many Americans, silence can be seen as a communication breakdown, and people will fill the silence with noise, even if they don't actually have anything important to say. The silence can lead to a sense of anxiety and fear that the conversation is failing.

I enjoy chatting with a friend from Brazil because she isn't very sensitive to interruptions. We finish each other's sentences, talk over each other and always have a fun and lively conversation. On the other hand, my German landlord, who I once rented an office space from, would have a visceral reaction if I ever interrupted and cut him off. My inattention to polite turn-taking was the height of rudeness. This is not to say that all Americans, Swedes, Brazilians and Germans will behave in these ways. You must be conscious of your relationship, the individual preferences of the person you are speaking with and the context of your conversation.

Understanding the individual preferences of people in your group or team and coming to agreements around *how* you communicate can help your group be more productive and effective in their interactions. Sit down with your team members to talk about each other's communication preferences and draft ground rules for your meetings and other communication channels.

When it's your turn to listen, do so with all your senses. We can show that we are listening by using three types of cues: visual, vocal and verbal. It's your job to decide what's best in your context and situation, based on what you know about the people you are speaking with.

Visual cues can be simple signals such as nodding your head, making appropriate eye contact, having attentive posture and using appropriate facial expressions and responses. Putting down your phone and closing your laptop are great ways to show that you are focused on the speaker. Vocal cues are short vocal responses, such as 'mm-hmm', 'oh, yeah', 'okay', 'right', 'wow', 'yes', etc. They are responses that show you are listening and reacting, but don't interrupt the flow of the speaker or redirect the conversation elsewhere.

Verbal cues refer to longer answers and responses to the speaker and they serve a specific function:

Function	Response
Acknowledging the speaker	'Thanks so much for sharing that'
Asking for clarification	'Could you please rephrase that?'
Checking for understanding	'So if I understand you correctly, you mean...'
Asking curious questions	'Could you tell me more about...?'

Listening in a digital age

In a world filled with so much noise, listening is becoming more important than ever. With algorithms deciding which information we see and from whom, we need to take more responsibility for seeking out and listening to multiple sides of a story.

We have a lot of power over what we see and hear through social media and can easily block and unfriend people we don't agree with or don't want to listen to. This can bring some relief in managing the amounts of information in our feeds. At the same time, it can further divide us, as we all retreat to our familiar, comfort zones where we interact with other people who think and behave the same way we do. Many of us are unintentionally cutting cognitive diversity from our circles and creating our own little digital echo chambers.

Advances in technology have multiplied our communication channels. It's not uncommon to be interacting with people on several different instant messaging platforms, such as email, an online project management programme, text messages, a customer relationship management or sales portal, as well as taking phone calls, joining meetings (live, virtual and hybrid) and meeting people for virtual coffees. Our attention has never been so divided in a time when we need to listen more consciously than ever.

Used correctly, these channels have their benefits. You can listen to a voice message several times to better understand someone's message before you craft a reply. It's easier to delete a message with errors (or heightened emotions) before the receiver reads it. We have ways to track who has read what. We get instant gratification from our communication.

On the other hand, technology brings its challenges. Bandwidth limitations can create poor call quality, and background noise can make it hard to understand a speaker. We've had to learn new ways to listen. When we sit in a face-to-face meeting, listening is a full-body sport. We watch subtle shifts in body language and listen for changes to the pace of speech and tone to know when a person has finished speaking and who might want to go next. In online settings, we lose most of the body language, especially the direction of gaze between speakers.

Where we look and who we look at often play a large role in turn-taking, signalling who is engaged with the speaker and who is interested in adding to the conversation. This is impossible to decipher online. You can't see who people are looking at on their screens, and you can't make eye contact in the same way either. We lose a lot of our communicative superpowers.

In learning to listen in new ways, there may be a silver lining. Virtual meetings have a slower pace out of necessity. Everything that is implicit when we sit face to face now needs to be explicit. We need to call on people to speak, unmute our microphones and decide when it's safe to start talking. This slower pace could have the positive result of giving us more time to think and more time to listen and process what others say. Still, many people report feelings of awkwardness and think conversations seem staged or unnatural. We dive deeper into managing some of these challenges in Chapter 15.

Listening to accents

In our global world, it is close to impossible to *not* speak with people who sound different than you. If you have difficulty understanding certain people on your team, or if your company is expanding into a particular global market, it is worth the time and effort to train your ear to recognize other accents.

You can do this by increasing your contact with the target accent. The more you hear an accent, the easier it becomes to understand it. Listen to a target accent as much as possible (find recorded sources such as talk radio, TED talks, podcasts, interviews with famous people, etc.) to tune your ear faster. Don't shy away from speaking to people you find difficult to understand. The more you speak to them, the better you'll get.

You can also look at accents as a puzzle or code. When English is not a person's first language, there will be sounds in English that don't exist in their native tongue. Since they do not know how to make those sounds, they will substitute them with another sound from their native language that sounds the most similar in their ears. What's great is that these substitutions are consistent.

Most languages don't have a 'TH' sound, for example. In English we actually have two. Compare 'bath' and 'bathe' to hear (and feel) the difference. A German speaker will substitute an 'S' or 'Z', respectively. Mandarin speakers will substitute 'T' or 'D', unless they come from Malaysia or Singapore. Then the 'TH' at the ends of words will turn to 'F' and 'V'. They'll do this every time. Crack the code of the accent, and it's much easier to understand.

Bad listening habits

Everyone I know likes to think that they are good listeners (myself included), but we all make listening mistakes, often without even realizing we're doing it. Our only goal when listening should be to connect and understand, but our minds are often consumed with many other activities and thoughts. Let's look at some of these bad habits and how to overcome them.

Listening to respond, instead of to understand

The fast-thinking brain is working constantly while we listen. It is organizing and classifying all the information we see and hear, and it is making judgements and assumptions based on patterns from our past.

It's up to us to use our slow-thinking brains to overcome that process while listening. You can't stop your brain from categorizing the information you hear, but your slow-thinking brain can choose not to pass judgement on it or reflect on it further.

The next time you are in a conversation, try to consciously watch your brain work. Yes, I realize that this will detract from your listening, but just try this as an experiment. As the speaker talks, you'll likely notice that you are processing the information, deciding whether you support or reject the information, and you are already considering your response. You might even notice that you are doing this now as you read. You are sorting through the words on the page, deciding if they make sense to you, if you have seen examples that support what you're reading, and you are deciding what is important and unimportant in your world view. All these things are also happening during conversations when you are supposed to be listening!

Raise your awareness while listening to stay focused on what the person is saying. Give them space to think and speak without passing judgement or formulating your response. Instead of responding with your views, ask for some clarification or further examples so you are sure you fully understand the topic of discussion from the speaker's perspective.

Finishing the speaker's thoughts

'We finish each other's sentences,' is often a declaration of love and connection that signals two people think in similar ways. Most people view this positively. However, trying to finish someone's sentence can often end in failure. If we are crossing languages and cultures, we have an even greater chance of finishing a sentence incorrectly. It's not your job to think for the speaker. As you try to make assumptions about where the speaker is going next, you miss what they are saying now.

Misinterpreting meaning

In global environments especially, everyone interprets words and phrases differently. Just because you use the same words doesn't mean you both have understood the meaning in the same way.

Creating meaning goes beyond words to an understanding of the concepts the words describe. Consider a word like 'respect'. When you hear the word, your mind will immediately start making connections to people and experiences in which you have shown respect, lost respect, felt respected/disrespected, and so on.

You might have a definition of respect that includes concepts such as trust and competence, meaning that you respect people whom you trust, who have high levels of competence. They could be younger or older, male or female. You'll also have ideas about how respect is shown: saying please and thank you, not interrupting, maintaining eye contact. Someone else could have very different associations to the word 'respect'. They might avoid eye contact to show respect, give respect to anyone who is older and never challenge their ideas.

If we want to get a deeper understanding of a speaker's meaning, it's important to listen to more than words. This may mean asking more questions, not making assumptions based on our own understandings of the world and keeping the world view of the speaker front of mind.

Using the same words to describe something does not necessarily mean that the meaning is the same.

One-upping

Have you ever told a meaningful story just to have the other person respond with a similar story of their own? It's like they think their story will better prove the point you are trying to make than yours.

This often backfires. When a listener does this, they don't typically mean to be one-upping the speaker. They are trying to demonstrate common experience with the intention of showing empathy for someone's situation. This kind of sharing has its place, especially when conveying vulnerability and building relationships. It's important, however, to make the speaker feel their experience has been acknowledged and not simply dismissed.

Solving the speaker's problem

We all want to help our friends, but some may forget that not everyone needs help. They just need to feel heard. Imagine that your friend is having a problem with her boss, husband, best friend, colleague, employee, child's teacher or someone else. Do you really listen to what she is saying and feeling or are you trying to think of some advice you can give, or a way to solve her problem? Sometimes people aren't looking for solutions. They're just looking for a good friend to listen and empathize.

In the field of executive coaching, the first rule every coach is taught is that they must have permission to coach someone. This is a great rule to follow when you find yourself wanting to give unsolicited advice. Ask for permission first. 'Would you like to brainstorm some solutions?' is a great way to offer your help. The speaker can decide if they wish to accept. Still, you shouldn't be thinking about how to help while you are listening. You can wait to offer assistance until after you've fully understood the situation and know the speaker wants to hear your opinion.

Letting emotion get in the way

One of the biggest challenges to rational thinking is a highly emotional response. If you are in a conversation, especially a conflict, and emotions begin to rise, it's difficult to listen with an open mind. Your emotions can begin to cloud your judgement. You might get defensive and begin taking things personally. This is when your ability to understand the speaker's perspective will be reduced.

To see the situation from the speaker's perspective needs a high level of cultural intelligence. Take a deep breath and refocus on the speaker's message. You will have plenty of time to process your own thoughts and feelings later. First, make sure you get the message straight.

Getting distracted

Distractions are everywhere, especially in our modern, digitally connected age. It's very easy to be distracted from listening carefully to others. You could be in a busy, noisy environment with distractions all around you. Perhaps you're distracted by the person – their appearance, clothing, something in their teeth, etc. You might stop thinking about what they're saying because you are admiring their accent or questioning their pronunciation or use of a particular word. You might have other thoughts on your mind that have nothing to do with the conversation. You could be distracted by your phone.

Before entering an important meeting, an interview or even a cocktail party, clear your mind of clutter and focus your energy on the people around you. Commit to being present. If you are thinking about the email you just read or the meeting you had that afternoon, your focus will not be on listening.

Press UNMUTE

- Develop systems to ensure equal talk time among the members of your team.
- Listening is a full-body sport. Communicate that you are listening through verbal, vocal and visual cues that are appropriate for the speaker's communicative culture and style.
- Become more aware of how you listen to others and do your best to break any bad listening habits that you might have.

5

🎙 Unmuted inclusion

'Oh! You didn't sound black on the phone...'[1]

'Noooo... Did he really say that?' I couldn't believe my ears. My friend and colleague, a black, female, American consultant based in Singapore, was dead serious. She had spoken to a potential client, the vice president of a multinational company, many times on the phone. When she finally met him at his office, this was the way he greeted her.

'What did you say?' I had no idea how I would respond to something like that. Having heard this line before, however, she was prepared. Half rolling her eyes she said, 'Oh really? What exactly does *black* sound like?'

That apparently stopped this (white) Englishman's fast-thinking brain in its tracks. He fumbled and apologized, suddenly realizing how totally inappropriate his comment had been.

This book would not be complete without talking about inclusion. The whole point of the unmuted culture is to speak up, be heard and understood, and empower others to do the same – *all* others.

Unmuted inclusion

The word for the type of interaction my friend experienced was not as widespread back then, but now we know it to be a microaggression. Racial microaggressions are brief, everyday exchanges that send denigrating messages to people of colour because they belong to a racial minority group.[2] In this chapter, I'll use the term 'microinequity' to refer to not only microaggressions but also derogatory remarks directed at any group or individual that feels overlooked or undervalued at work (or anywhere else).

We can all believe that we are not racist, sexist, ageist or hold any other prejudice, but remember how the fast-thinking brain works. It filters and processes millions of bits of information and categorizes it based on patterns. It will always favour the patterns it sees the most. By default, it will work against minorities and maintain the master narratives we've been taught.

This is why microinequities are so often unintentional, and we may not even recognize them when they fly out of our mouths. Most of us don't want to believe we could be capable of saying something disparaging or behaving in a non-inclusive way. We want to believe we are good people. Most of us are, but we need to slow down our thinking (and our mouths) to become more conscious communicators.

This doesn't mean you can just blame your brain for using microinequities. What's important is to become aware when they happen, address them and stop them. This is the only way to break the cycle. I can guarantee that we have all been guilty of this at some point, even as minorities.

And microinequities are only part of the inclusion conversation. It is not just how we speak but, as discussed in Chapter 4, also how we listen that determines whether we are being truly inclusive.

Identifying microinequities

Microinequities can be difficult to spot. Those in the dominant, majority group won't usually recognize or be affected by them. When you're part of the 'in crowd' and don't deviate from cultural norms, it is hard to understand the experiences of those who are different. If someone takes offence to an off-handed comment, they are often accused of being overly sensitive. The person who said it will say that 'they didn't mean it like that'. Regardless of the intention, microinequities have the same consequence: certain individuals feel like outsiders and less worthy than the majority group.

Once we raise our awareness about what microinequities are, it gets easier to spot them. They are comments that point out the 'otherness' of another person or detract from their message by focusing on a personal trait. Microinequities make people feel like they are not part of the group and their ideas are not appreciated. Here are some examples of comments and behaviours that could be seen as non-inclusive:

Comments

- 'You all kind of look the same' (referring to ethnicity).
- 'You speak so well' (most people of your ethnicity, race or language background don't).
- 'He's [of a certain religion], but very open-minded' (most of that religion aren't).
- 'Is that your real hair?' (professional people don't look like that).
- 'Say that again! I love your accent!' (condescending focus on accent instead of message).
- 'Do you have a nickname?' (your name is so different – you should make it easier for us).

Behaviours

- Giving unequal attention to a certain dominant group of people.
- Constantly interrupting minorities.
- Only calling on people like you to speak.
- Uneven consideration of opinions.

Be aware of your preconceptions

Hearing, listening and including are three different things. Hearing someone speak is not the same as listening to their message. In turn, listening to a message does not mean that you have given it equal merit to all others. Your perceptions of the person speaking will influence your opinion of what they say. If you've made a decision about the credibility of the individual before they even begin to speak (usually based on completely subjective and prejudicial factors), their words may have no chance of making any impact.

This is the difference between a muted and an unmuted team. Regardless of what you think of a person (and regardless of the reasons you think that way), can you listen with a curious and open mind without letting *your* prejudices and assumptions influence *their* ideas?

There are always people we just don't like. It doesn't matter what they say, you'll probably find a problem with it. Conversely, you might have extra appreciation for your friend's ideas, missing their disjointed argument or lack of logic. Your relationship and connection to someone who thinks, acts and probably also looks more like you changes the way you judge what they say.

If you want to gain from the unique talents and viewpoints of everyone in the room, you must be incredibly honest with yourself. When you make a judgement, challenge it. Have a devil's advocate in your mind to run tests on your own logic. You might think you're unbiased, but none of us are.

Another unconscious bias that we are plagued with is the halo effect, which causes us to respond more positively to the first ideas we hear, especially if they are spoken by someone of whom we think highly. If you bring up an idea for discussion on your team, it's likely that the most confident and assertive people will speak first. The strong impression they make will then lead others to agree with these remarks instead of challenging them. They probably won't challenge them because their thinking has already been influenced. If you want to take advantage of the true cognitive diversity of your group, ask everyone to write down their ideas and opinions before anyone speaks. Then share what has been written on each person's paper to ensure their original opinions haven't been swayed by the halo effect.

Diversity is more than demographics

There are three different kinds of diversity: demographic, experiential and cognitive.[3] The one we hear about the most is demographic diversity, probably because it's the easiest to measure. Race, age, gender, sexual orientation and language are all demographic measures that form one part of our identities. Experiential diversity refers to personal interests, hobbies and abilities, many of which we can see on the culture wheel in Chapter 3. Finally, cognitive diversity refers to our differences in thinking styles and is probably the most difficult to measure. Since this is invisible, it is also the easiest to suppress. Research shows that cognitive diversity has the biggest positive impact on ideation and innovation in teams.[4] If we hire people who all look different but still think the same, our demographic diversity won't have our intended effect. This is one reason studies on diversity show little link between demographic diversity and increased economic returns for organizations.[5]

Hiring for diversity has become a cornerstone of recruitment, but the problems begin after you've formed your perfectly diverse team. Once a new hire starts in a company, they are quickly expected to conform to the company culture and fit in. There are many subjective markers of company culture that the new hire is expected to adapt to. Everything from changing their communication style to fit their boss or team to adopting a 'stronger work ethic' (e.g. 60-hour weeks) places pressure on new hires to fit in. Those who choose not to fit in have a much higher chance of leaving or being fired within the first 18 months.[6] If you want to reap the benefits of a cognitively diverse workplace, you have to develop a culture that is comfortable with difference.

If new employees feel more pressure to conform than contribute, their voices aren't heard and they don't feel included in the conversation. It makes absolutely no difference how diverse your demographics might be. If people aren't encouraged to show up and speak up, your diversity and inclusion agenda has moved from a human resources function to a public relations function. You are not walking the talk.

Awareness in action

Conscious communication has inclusion at its core. We must all be committed to recognizing, identifying and ending non-inclusive practices in the workplace.

To increase inclusion, raise awareness and draw attention to microinequities, give your teams the language and vocabulary to address these issues. Discuss examples of microinequities and educate each other about what they look and sound like. Make it okay to call out microinequities by explaining that they are learning opportunities. The majority of people are not purposely non-inclusive. It's important to recognize microinequities when they happen, so everyone is aware and acknowledging them.

Prioritize inclusion even higher than diversity. Diversity of ideas and opinions is worthless if they are never heard. Make sure that everyone is given equal time in meetings to express their views and avoid the halo effect by writing down ideas and opinions before the meeting even starts. Practise conscious listening when people speak to ensure you give equal merit to all ideas and not just the people to whom you are closest. You will need to listen even more attentively to the people you don't like.

Inclusion is an ongoing process that takes constant attention and effort. That effort pays off in innovation and efficiency when everyone feels like an equal and valued member of the team.

Press UNMUTE

- Learn more about unconscious biases and microinequities and the way they impact your team.
- Make it safe to identify and talk about microinequities in the moment they happen.
- Keep an open mind and listen consciously to everyone on your team.
- Give space for others to show up authentically. Embrace and celebrate differences in thought, mannerisms, appearance and interests.
- Get the most from the unique talents of your team members by walking the talk and not expecting conformity.

🎤 PART II: SPEAK UP

Confident Communication

🎙 Find your confidence

'I ask if there are questions and everyone says, "No". Then, within 30 minutes of the meeting ending, my inbox is full of their questions and comments.'

'That's more common than you'd think,' I replied. 'It's not that they don't have anything to say. They just don't want to say it to anyone but you.'

As flattering as it was for my client to hear this, she was still frustrated with her regional team's inability to speak up. She is part of the executive leadership team in a fast-paced, Big-4 consulting firm. She doesn't have the time to hold important meetings just so she can then be swamped with emails, forced to hold individual follow-up meetings, and then call another meeting to communicate the new information back out to the team. It was quickly becoming a vicious cycle with no end in sight.

There isn't a one-size-fits-all solution. Our 'willingness to communicate'[1] can be affected by many different factors: situational, motivational, cultural, and personal being just a few.

There are many hurdles to overcome before we can genuinely and authentically share our thoughts with confidence.

Some people have more confidence than others, but even the most confident doubt themselves at times. Perhaps you are very confident and think this chapter isn't for you, but I would encourage you to keep reading so you can develop a better understanding of some of your colleagues, friends and family members.

In this chapter we'll look at the types of confidence we need to cultivate and how to overcome our fears so we can unmute ourselves and help others to do the same.

Confidence in your skills

Most people I work with think the problem with their communication is their skill set. They lack confidence in their communicative competencies and believe that they do not have the capability to speak up well.

- 'I'm not a natural speaker.'
- 'I don't know how to give feedback.'
- 'I can't organize my thoughts fast enough.'
- 'I always blank out.'
- 'I'm not good at telling stories.'
- 'I speak bad English.'
- 'My accent is too heavy.'
- 'I make a lot of mistakes.'

Like a sport, they feel that if they train long and hard enough, they will overcome their flaws and this will give them the confidence to perform better. If all you are missing is confidence in your skills, then that's a simple fix. It's a training gap that can be filled. This is what most human resources departments are looking for when they find trainers and coaches for their top leaders and teams.

There are always ways to improve how we speak, whether it's articulating clearly in global environments, improving language skills or learning more impactful presentation techniques. We'll touch on some of these communicative competencies in the following chapters.

Any high-performing athlete will tell you: the challenges to perform go deeper than physical ability or competence. Focusing on skill sets is easy; we just tick the boxes. You could have all the skills in the world, but if you don't have the confidence in yourself to apply those skills or if you have anxiety around your ability to perform, the skills themselves are worthless.

To build self-confidence, we must look at the way we think about ourselves and the way we communicate, not just how we communicate. The real problem is in our minds, not our mouths.

Confidence in yourself

It's very natural to feel vulnerable when you speak up in front of a group. We all want to feel like we belong and like our contributions are appreciated. We want to avoid embarrassment and be respected for our talents and ideas. Speaking up puts us in a situation where all or one of these things could go wrong.

My clients express a number of fears regarding speaking up in their organizations. What triggers one person's self-doubt could be very different from another person. Here are some of the most common fears I hear:

Table 6.1 Common Speaking Fears

Fear	What It Sounds Like
Judgement	'They won't take me seriously.'
Rejection	'They won't want to work with me.'
Not 'good enough'	'My ideas aren't important. I don't deserve a place at the table.'
Embarrass self and/or others	'I don't want to make a mistake.' 'I don't want to make the boss look bad.'
Losing one's job	'They'll fire me if I speak up.'

These fears will vary according to the individual, their culture, position in an organization and a number of other factors. They will change in importance throughout one's life and career as well. If I see someone who has just joined an organization and is trying to make a good impression, fear of embarrassment is probably at the top of their list. This fear could be equally strong for a CEO who must address the board of directors (yes, even CEOs get scared), but maybe their fear of judgement is even stronger since their success will depend on how much the board respects them.

Expression anxiety

Fear triggers anxiety. This is the nervousness we feel when we need to make a big presentation, introduce ourselves at a networking event or even speak to people we do not know. This anxiety can show up with an audience of any size, from one person to thousands. You could even experience the same anxiety when you need to send an important email, publicly post your opinion on social media or write an article or book.

Typically referred to as 'speaking anxiety', I prefer to call this 'expression anxiety' because you can experience it any time you try to unmute and express yourself, whether speaking or writing.

Everyone responds to expression anxiety differently. If you tend to suffer from anxiety in general, you might see these responses in other situations as well. Harrison Monarth and Larina Kase categorize our responses into four areas: biological, behavioural, cognitive and emotional.[2] Biological responses refer to physical responses that you cannot control – a racing heart or shaking hands are good examples. These differ from behavioural responses, which are nervous tics that you can control if you are aware of them. Clicking your pen or playing with your hair or clothing would be behavioural expressions of your anxiety. Cognitive responses refer to the (usually negative) thoughts running through your mind, and emotional responses have to do with your feelings of self-worth in the moment.

In the table below, consider which responses resonate with your experiences and think of any additional responses you might add to the list.

Table 6.2 Responses to Expression Anxiety

Biological *Your body responds with:*	Cognitive *You think:*
shaking hands	'This is going to be horrible.'
sweaty palms/excessive body sweat	'I can't do this.'
blushing face	'They're going to judge me.'
rapid/shallow breathing	'I'm not prepared.'
racing heart	'I'm going to look stupid.'
shaking knees/legs	'I don't know what I'm talking about.'
dry mouth	'My content isn't good enough.'
upset stomach	'I can't/won't find the words.'
need to use the restroom	'They'll never understand me.'

Behavioural	Emotional
You display these nervous behaviours:	*You feel:*
Playing with your hair	Anxious
Adjusting your clothing (tie, belt, skirt, top)	Depressed
Clicking a pen	Embarrassed
Crazy laser pointer	Worried
Scratching	Tense
Touching your face	Panicky
Making excuses to avoid the situation	Upset
Stiffness	Nervous
Hiding your hands behind your back	Worthless
Excessive movement or swaying	Helpless
Tapping your foot	

These responses can come in any order. For example, maybe you are feeling nervous (emotional) about an upcoming talk. This initiates an adrenaline response that makes your hands shake (biological). You stand stiffly with your hands behind your back (behavioural) so that people don't notice. Then you think: 'I shouldn't even be here. I don't know what I'm talking about' (cognitive). This then triggers another emotional response of worthlessness, and now you've fallen deep down the spiral of expression anxiety.

In another example, you need to write an article on a topic that is really important to you. You sit down to write, but you can't find the words. All you can think about is how everyone is going to judge you and try to tear you apart. You know your message is important but are you sure? Is your message good enough? (cognitive). You can feel your hands getting sweaty on your keyboard (biological), and then you get up to walk around and let out some nervous energy (behavioural). You make an excuse about something else you need to do and avoid writing (behavioural). As time passes, you feel more worthless (emotional) because you still haven't done what you committed to do. It gets harder and harder to get started.

What's holding you back?

There are many factors that influence how willing we are to speak. We might be completely comfortable in some situations, but struggle in others. Consider how the following factors: audience, time, language and topic make you feel more nervous about expressing yourself. Do you feel anxiety relating to your skill set, or is it a deeper anxiety that is tied to self-worth? Notice how ridiculous some of the descriptions sound when you are thinking logically and rationally about the situation.

1. Audience
Size of audience
Do you prefer to speak up in front of big or small audiences? How big is 'big'? Imagine you've been asked to speak in front of five people. Is that okay for you? What about 15, 50, 500? Which number starts to trigger your anxiety? What about when you write? If you need to send an email to the whole department, do you feel more nervous than when you send it to just one person? Do you feel your anxiety build as you produce content on social media and your audience starts growing bigger and bigger?

Relationship with audience
Maybe the size of the audience has no effect on you, but the people in it do. Is there anyone in particular (a family member, boss, someone you admire, someone you have a difficult history with) who makes you more nervous than others? Are you afraid of them judging or rejecting you? Maybe you're worried that what you say isn't good enough and will cause you embarrassment. Or maybe they'll trigger your impostor syndrome and you'll fear they'll discover that you don't know what you're talking about.

Age
Do you feel more confident working with children and students, but have difficulty expressing yourself among peers? Is it the opposite? Are there certain age groups that you find particularly intimidating?

Belonging

How much do you have in common with the people you are speaking or writing to? Are you from the same culture? Do you have a similar education? Do you speak the same language? Are you a member of this particular group or are you addressing people very different from you? Are you worried about how they will respond to your ideas? How accepted do you feel by your audience, or are you unknown to them?

Security

Do you feel psychologically safe in this environment, or do you fear that your job could be in jeopardy if you speak up and unmute? We'll look at psychological safety and how to build collaborative environments in Part III.

Solutions for audience concerns

When you find yourself getting nervous about your audience, whether it is the size, the people in it, their ages, your sense of belonging, feelings of safety in the group, or any other audience-related issue, there is a very quick fix. Get out of your head and focus on the impact you can make on the lives of these people. Your presentation is not about you. It is about them. The great majority of audience members want to see you succeed. They have asked you to share your ideas for a reason. Embrace this.

2. Time

Preparation time

Do you feel more at ease when you are given lots of time to prepare? Do you find that it doesn't matter how much time you're given, because you'll wait until the last minute anyway? Do you often find yourself worrying that you don't have enough time? Do you use time as an excuse for a poor presentation or written document?

Length of presentation or writing
Do you get more anxious when you must produce a lot or a little bit of information? Is a five-minute presentation harder for you to prepare than a one-hour presentation? Is it easier for you to focus on writing a 500-word article than a 50,000-word book?

Solutions for concerns about time
It's rare that we feel we've been given enough time to prepare for a presentation or finish an important report. The reality is, whether you are given months or just a few days, if you have a habit of procrastinating, it probably doesn't matter how much time you're given.

What if your problem actually has nothing to do with time? Dr Tim Pychyl, member of the Procrastination Research Group at Carleton University explains that 'procrastination is an emotion-regulation problem, not a time-management problem'.[3] You avoid the task at hand because it creates negative emotions. You feel anxious and overwhelmed and don't know where to start. Or at least that's what you tell yourself.

Try to think about what your next step *could* be if you were to start the project. Maybe you would open a new PowerPoint presentation. Or you would find the file dealing with this project and read through it. Those simple steps don't feel so scary or hard. Your motivation to do the task only comes once you start. So just get started. Inspiration will strike and your self-confidence will grow.

3. Language
Fluency
How fluent are you in the language you need to express yourself in? If English is not your first language and you need to formally present or write in that language for an international audience, do you believe in your ability to do so?

Fluency of audience

Do you feel comfortable speaking or writing in a foreign language to other foreign-language speakers? Is it easier for you to speak with native speakers of that language?

Solutions for language concerns

Language concerns can be a big hindrance for many international professionals. With English the global language of business, non-native speakers can feel like they are at a disadvantage. In reality, it is often the native speaker that is the most misunderstood. We'll look at language very closely in Chapters 9 and 10, but the best way to overcome some of these basic concerns is to practise your presentation out loud (or read your writing out loud). Find the words you need. Practise the phrases you'll need to use. Check any definitions, spellings or pronunciations you are unsure about. Ask a colleague to review your slides for spelling or grammatical errors (even if you did a spell check). This advice is good for all English speakers, not just ones who have English as an additional language.

4. Topic

Your expertise

Do you feel as if you really know the topic? Are you confident in your knowledge? Do you think you aren't good enough to talk about this subject, or question why someone asked you to do so? Surely there must be someone better suited for the job! Impostor syndrome is a common concern for many high-achieving professionals.

Solutions for thinking you don't know enough

If you don't have the information you need, research or ask colleagues for support. If the problem is perfectionism, remember that you were asked to speak up for a reason. Someone believed in you and your message. Remember that self-doubt is normal and no one has all the answers all the time. We're all learning. Just because you say or write something today, doesn't mean you can't change your mind tomorrow.

Before you can really speak up with confidence, you need to know exactly what is holding you back. Then you can work on developing the skills confidence and self-confidence you need to truly unmute. Don't make the common mistake of thinking that all you need are more skills. If you don't work on the underlying fears that are crippling your self-confidence, none of the skills will really help you!

Press UNMUTE

- Identify your biological, behavioural, cognitive and emotional reactions to expression anxiety.
- Determine what is triggering your expression anxiety and find ways to mitigate these triggers.
- Identify what is holding you back from expressing yourself with confidence and watch for those signals so that you can stop them in their tracks.
- Recognize that there is always a risk in unmuting. Remember that the importance of your message outweighs the risk.

🎙 Body language from a box

'Do I *really* need to tell my people to get dressed for meetings?'

'Yes. Yes, you do,' I replied in a sarcastic voice, matching the eye-roll reaction I could feel radiating from this regional manager during the height of COVID-19-induced virtual meeting mayhem.

He was struggling to get his team to participate with the same professionalism they would typically show in the office. People would show up in T-shirts that they may or may not have worn to bed the night before. They sat in front of open doors to bathrooms, had piles of junk, laundry or other inappropriate things behind them in the frame and didn't seem to show any awareness of their surroundings.

'These people are having calls with our clients!' he exclaimed.

This was just one of the common problems we faced when the world went online almost overnight in early 2020. Even more pressing was figuring out how to motivate and engage a suddenly remote team. How could we possibly feel the energy of human connection through technology and survive being squeezed into a little box on a screen?

But of course, we did. We found ways to communicate and connect just as we have over the telephone, in emails and text messages and through social media. This time we had the added benefit of being able to see each other on camera as well.

Microsoft studied the data from more than 30,000 Microsoft 365 and LinkedIn users in 31 countries and published their findings in the 2021 Work Trend Index.[1] They found that teams were *more* connected at the beginning of the pandemic, not less. People had more contact with their close networks, while they drastically reduced contact to their larger networks.

In the beginning of our transition to video-enabled communication platforms, you only had to be slightly good with technology to make a positive impression online. Not many people knew what they were doing, and everyone was very forgiving. We expected technical difficulties, assumed people would have issues with their cameras and microphones, and few people dressed as they would in the office (to the great frustration of my client).

If nothing else, virtual communication levelled the playing field. It cut the charisma of overly dominant speakers and put more focus on content-rich conversation. On the other hand, it also made it easier for some people to disengage and hide. Camera off and muted, they could disappear without others noticing as easily.

Over a year later, at the time of this writing, there's one thing we know: on-camera communication is here to stay. It's time to unmute and be seen on camera, and we need to build the confidence to do this well.

Every time I think we all must know this by now, I hear another shocking story from a client about a meeting or online conference where their industry colleagues or competitors showed up unprofessionally on camera. Knowing how to carry your professional presence into the online space sets you apart. Let's make sure you are noticed for the right reasons.

Making a great first impression

What's wrong with this picture? If you thought 'Just about everything', you are right. Think about how you show up for in-person events and meetings. Whether you know the people or not, you dress a certain way, use eye contact appropriately, offer a firm handshake (or the appropriate greeting in your part of the world) and introduce yourself. Why do many of these basic manners fail to translate online?

Some people quietly enter online meetings without announcing themselves. They keep their cameras off and wait to be addressed. I don't think these people mean to be rude. They just feel uncomfortable and, in some cases vulnerable, as they sit in their makeshift home offices (their bedrooms). It's not exactly the professional image they want to send.

These images and the accompanying table demonstrate how small adjustments can make a huge difference to your professional presence online.

Table 7.1 Your Professional Presence Online

Before	After
Face is too dark	Face is well lit
Too much backlight	Light shining from front
No grooming, improper dress	Professional grooming and clothing
Camera is angled upwards	Camera is positioned at eye level
Poor framing	Framing follows an amended rule of thirds
No eye contact	Eye contact with the camera
Distracting background	Clean, organized background
No external microphone or headset	External microphone headset used for better sound and reduced echo
No gestures can be seen	Gestures are within the frame

Let's take a closer look at some simple adjustments we can make in each area:

Lighting

Just as when you are taking a photograph, light needs to shine on the main object of attention. In this case, it's your face. If you must sit with a window behind you, close the curtains and place a light source in front of you. Don't underestimate what you already have. For most work situations, simple standing lamps in your house will be good enough.

If you want better lighting or have a more formal presentation to do, such as at a conference, there are many affordable options for small LED or ring lights that can clip on to your computer monitor. These are a great quick fix, especially if you need to show up online in the early mornings or evenings to fit in with global time zones.

If you wear glasses, anti-glare coating will be a good investment, but even then, you will still need to avoid light shining directly into your face. Taller LED lights or a photography soft box might be a better alternative for you if you can't sit facing a window or need to take calls when it is dark outside.

Grooming and dress

It's simple. Show up online the same way you would face to face. If it's not appropriate in the office, it's not appropriate in the home office either. If you would have shaved this morning before going to the office, you should probably shave before your client call. If you typically wear make-up to work, make the same effort in an online meeting with your colleagues.

Framing and camera placement

One very simple and powerful way you can improve your online presence is to reposition your laptop or monitor so that you are properly framed and can look straight into your camera.

If you are using a laptop that sits on your table or desk, the built-in camera will naturally be much lower than your eye level. In this situation, you might angle the laptop upwards so that your face can be seen. However, this is a very unflattering view that normally includes multiple chins and up-the-nostrils shots.

A simple fix is to place your laptop on a pile of books, or better still invest in a proper stand for your laptop. This makes your workspace more ergonomic and allows for a more direct line of sight into your camera.

When your camera is at the right level, you'll want to think about where to place yourself in the frame. In art and photography, the 'rule of thirds' is used to position objects in a composition so that they appeal to us most. This artistic guideline divides a frame with two horizontal lines and two vertical lines in order to create nine equal sections. When we view images, our eyes naturally gravitate to these invisible lines and their intersections. A 'good' composition places objects of interest along these lines, and especially at the intersections of the lines.

Even those who know about the rule of thirds often forget about it when they log into virtual meetings. They centre their eyes in the middle of the screen with a lot of empty space above their heads. A more balanced composition lifts the eyes up to the top third line. This has the added benefit of showing more of the torso, so you can also include gestures in the frame.

If we really follow the rule of thirds, we will also position ourselves on the right or left third line, but this doesn't work so well in online meetings. Several video-conferencing platforms automatically cut off the sides of your picture when multiple cameras are on and we are in gallery view. I suggest you position yourself in the centre of the frame (vertically), so when people change their screen view, you are still fully visible.

Eye contact

One of the hidden benefits of online video conferencing is that you have the ability to make eye contact with all your audience members at the same time. Instead of splitting your gaze between a group of people in a meeting room or auditorium, you're having an intimate one-to-one conversation with each person. You are sitting with them on their sofa, at their desk or around the dining room table. This offers the opportunity for you to make a completely different (and deeper) impact on everyone – if done well.

The science of gaze (where we look, when and for how long) in social situations is a very complex area of study. What we typically think of as making eye contact is actually 'face scanning', where the angle of our gaze moves small degrees to take in visual cues from the whole face of the person we're speaking with.[2] This is why proper framing and camera placement are so important. To receive the complete message, we need to be able to see the full face (not just someone's forehead at the bottom of a poorly angled laptop).

Our natural tendency when speaking on a video call is to look at each individual person. We talk to them on the screen and watch their reactions, forgetting that, from their perspective, we're not actually looking at them at all. The only way to look at our listeners in a way that they will feel our gaze is to look directly into our cameras.

This creates a number of challenges. It's very unnatural to stare into a 'black hole' or a green dot while trying to connect with people. Unless you have a background in television broadcasting, connecting through a camera can be an uncomfortable and disconnected experience at first. It takes practice to get good at it.

I find it helps to place a picture of a loved one near my camera, which draws my eyes back to this focal point. Perhaps you can envision the person you are speaking with in your mind's eye. The idea is to get that emotional connection going, even though you aren't looking at the person's face.

Like a real black hole, it might feel as if the camera is sucking in all your energy while giving nothing back. But you don't have to stare at the camera all the time, just like you wouldn't make constant eye contact with a person right in front of you.

The level and duration of direct eye contact vary greatly from culture to culture. Look at the camera in the same way that you would typically look into a person's eyes. Instead of looking at the screen when you want to make eye contact, look at the camera. It's okay to look away and think, direct your gaze to the chat box or to change a slide in your presentation. If you are worried about making 'too much' eye contact, remember that your listeners will decide whether they look back into your eyes or not. People who are uncomfortable with eye contact will focus their gaze on another part of your face (under the eyes, the nose or mouth) or will look away from the screen at their notes or something else without even thinking about it.

Background

Your background can say a lot about you if you want it to. When we are able to peek into each other's homes and meet family members and pets for the first time, we can end up feeling closer to our colleagues. For relaxed team meetings, informal (and even messy) backgrounds can build trust and connection.

For more formal presentations or external meetings, a simple, clean background is important. I saw a high-level professional deliver a global webinar for his industry association from his bedroom with the bathroom door open behind him. This did not give a professional impression.

Even for informal meetings, however, not everyone is comfortable inviting colleagues into their homes. This is when you could use a professional, company-approved, branded virtual background. Many organizations are now pre-loading these virtual backgrounds in their company-wide communication system. Think of it as a free marketing opportunity, plus it prevents people from showing up to important presentations next to palm trees on a virtual beach.

When using virtual backgrounds, watch out for disappearing fingers and arms or strange moving halos of colour around you. To avoid this, sit in front of a plain wall or use a green screen behind you. Many companies are now building green screen studios for employees who need to present in an online or hybrid environment. As we transition to even more virtual communication, this will prove to be money well spent.

Sound

The quality of your sound is more important than ever. Invest in a good headset with a microphone to cut any echo, and make sure your voice is as clear as possible. Check your sound settings on both your computer and your online platform to ensure that you are using the correct microphone and that your voice is not too loud or too soft. When you use a microphone, you don't need to project your voice the same way that you would in person.

Communicating without words

We say a lot with our hands, bodies and faces when we communicate. If you tend to use gestures, remember to keep them in your frame. You will need to bring your gestures up to shoulder level, which might feel a bit odd at first. If you forget to do this, none of your gestures will be seen, and it will just look like you are dancing in your chair.

If you use a web camera, this will often distort the image, making anything closer to the camera appear much bigger. If you lean forward towards the camera or reach your hands too far in front of you towards your screen, you'll end up with a larger-than-life forehead or finger.

If you are using a virtual background without a green screen, you might need to decrease the intensity of your gestures. Depending on the platform and the quality of your Internet connection, your appendages could disappear if you move too much, too quickly.

If, like me, you tend to express a lot of emotion with your face, remember that when your camera is on. It's easy to get so comfortable in your own private workspace that you forget that people are watching. If you are listening to a presentation and have a negative physical reaction to something someone says, there could be people in the group who see you!

Your posture also communicates your level of interest in a subject. Sit or stand as you would in a face-to-face meeting. Slouching over your desk or propping your head up with your hand doesn't send the best message to the presenter. If you're worried about your energy dropping, try to stand up at a high table during the call.

Energy management is crucial, because just as a camera adds 10 pounds of weight, it also cuts your energy significantly. You'll need to be more animated than normal to hold people's attention. Show your enthusiasm and your passion – and remember to smile when appropriate.

What we don't see

Management consultant Peter Drucker said in a 1989 interview, 'The most important thing in communication is to hear what isn't being said.'[3] With online communication we can add 'and see what isn't being shown'.

Being online has changed the dynamics of our visual communication. Much of our message can easily be hidden outside our screen, such as a tapping foot, sweaty palms or a shaky hand. When you check in with people, use all your senses to read their signs. Listen to their voices and the words they use. Notice the way they sit and their overall demeanour. Just as you can hear whether someone is smiling on the telephone, you will also be able to read the mood of your room, but you'll need to look carefully, in a way you haven't before.

Press UNMUTE

- Show up online with the same professionalism, confidence and credibility as you would in a face-to-face meeting or presentation.
- Use what you have. There is no need to invest in a pricey studio to make a fabulous impression online. Good sound, a camera at eye level and lighting in front of you are all you really need.
- When you want to make eye contact with someone, remember to look in the camera and not at their eyes on the screen.

🎙 A voice that flows like honey

'I strive for mellifluity.'
Siri's reply when I asked her if she liked her voice

Seriously, Siri? 'Hey Siri… What does "mellifluity" mean?'

I didn't expect this exchange with Siri to be such a learning experience, nor that she would offer such perfect fodder for this chapter. 'Mellifluity' is a made-up word – a nominalization of the adjective 'mellifluous', meaning 'pleasingly smooth and musical to hear'. The word's Latin etymology offers a beautiful metaphor. It means 'flowing like honey' and was most commonly used in the early seventeenth century.

This response was interesting to me for a couple of reasons. We humans often nominalize verbs and adjectives, creating words that your English teacher at school probably wouldn't have accepted. Think about the newer practice of sending an 'invite' instead of inviting someone to an event. This is an example of nominalization. When I watched Siri draw on artificial intelligence to produce such a human-like reaction, it reminded me how human our technology is becoming. If it weren't for her synthetic voice, Siri might have had me fooled.

And this was the second thing I found interesting. Even when a machine can deliver a human-like reply, we will almost always be able to tell that the voice is synthetic, even if we can't say exactly why. As technology advances, this could very well change, but modelling a human voice is an incredibly complex process.

Our voices could be the single most important tool we have for empathetic human connection. Social psychologist Michael Kraus, of Yale School of Management, carried out a number of experiments that showed just how powerful our voices are for conveying emotion. He concluded that we could identify someone's emotional state more accurately when we remove visual cues and only listen to the voice.[1]

This could explain the popularity of new audio-only social media apps. These apps are too new at the time of writing for me to attempt to declare a winner. There are already three serious contenders. Many users of these apps (myself included) report feeling a deep, more authentic connection to people (usually complete strangers) in a very short time. The connections are much stronger than ones built through text-based communication on social media networking sites like LinkedIn or Facebook.

Vocal cues that make a difference

We have many ways of adding additional meaning to our messages with our voices. We don't only vocalize content through language. We also use paralanguage (elements that go beyond language). The cues that I will discuss here are pitch, volume, tempo, intonation and resonance.

Pitch

Your pitch is not one specific tone but rather a range, and it varies according to age and gender. It can even have substantial fluctuations during the course of a day. You might notice that, when you are happy or excited, you speak faster and your pitch is higher. If you have less energy, you will probably speak with a lower pitch. Still, we usually stay within two or three octaves unless we unnaturally push our voices outside of normal range.

There could be reasons why people artificially change their voices, despite it being dangerous to the delicate vocal organs. We know that a certain pitch can exude certain qualities. A lower pitch is perceived as more masculine, authoritative and confident. A higher pitch is seen as more feminine, caring and friendly.

This is just one of the links between voice and gender bias. Can a woman hold a position of authority if she has a soft, higher-pitched voice? Will she demand the respect she deserves? Many have heard the popular story of Margaret Thatcher using a voice coach to lower her pitch in order be more competitive in her male-dominated world. There seems to be little evidence that this was the case.

In her book *The Human Voice,* Anne Karpf documents an interview she conducted with Tim Bell, the advertising executive Thatcher hired to run her campaign publicity.[2] Bell dismissed the idea that Thatcher had any type of formal coaching. If she had, he knew nothing about it.

He explained very clearly that he and a couple of advisers (all men) personally worked with Thatcher to change her voice, accent and communication style.

Karpf explains that while women's overall pitch dropped significantly over the four decades between 1980 and 2010, Thatcher managed to make the same change to her voice in just one decade. By forcing an artificial change, there is a good chance that she permanently damaged her vocal folds.

In a more recent example, many have speculated about the voice of Elizabeth Holmes, the former founder of now defunct medical company Theranos. In the book *Bad Blood,* which chronicles the rise and fall of the fraudulent founder and her company, author John Carreyrou says that Holmes' deep voice was just part of her fraud.[3] He has several sources that report hearing her fall out of character. Perhaps she felt, like Thatcher's advisers, that another way to gain credibility and compete in a world of male tech professionals was to lower her voice.

Pitch tips
- Get to know your voice and its natural range.
- Do not force your voice higher or lower than this natural range.
- Use your range purposefully. Move to a lower (natural) pitch when you are making an important point or need to show authority.

Use tones higher in your pitch range to express friendliness and excitement.

Volume

Learning to vary your volume can help you to make even more impact when speaking. Loud is not always best, and sometimes you can get the most attention when you lower your voice so much that people need to lean in to hear your next words.

Volume modulation is an essential skill to master. If you're always too loud, you can be seen as overly dominant and attention-seeking. On the other hand, if you speak too softly, you might be seen as insecure, shy and lacking in confidence.

All our vocal cues are also influenced by culture. Americans the world over are known for being loud in public places. You can often hear the American in the international restaurant, waiting room or airport lounge – even from across the room. Finding a good balance for your situation is important, and having common courtesy is key.

Volume tips

- Read the room. Are you the loudest one there? Turn down your volume.
- If you do need to speak with a louder voice, be sure that you are using your voice effectively and supporting your voice with your breath. Project your voice, don't yell.

Tempo

The speed at which you speak can have a huge effect on not only how intelligible you are but also how your voice sounds. The faster you speak, the higher your pitch becomes. You can also come across as sounding anxious, nervous and stressed if you speak too quickly.

Speeding up your speech is a natural reaction to nervous and anxious feelings. The sooner you get all your words out, the sooner you can end whatever terrible experience you are in: speaking in public, sitting in an interview or meeting someone on a blind date, for example.

Speaking too slowly is no better. You could be perceived as being boring, uneducated or incompetent. If you speak too slowly, you'll likely sound very monotone as well. If your pitch goes too low, it won't resonate well. You might sound as though you are too tired to speak properly.

Your tempo will change naturally according to your emotions. If you're nervous, it will typically speed up, although in cases of extreme anxiety, it might cause you to speak much slower. Get in touch with your emotions and begin to understand the effect they have on your pace of delivery. Then you can use tempo to your advantage, speeding up to sound more excited and passionate, and slowing down when you want to show control and seriousness.

Tempo tips

- Change your pace during a presentation to grab attention. When you suddenly speed up or slow down, people will notice and wonder what is coming next.
- Don't be afraid to pause. Pauses give your listener the chance to absorb your message, and they can also be used for dramatic effect.

Intonation

The melody of your speech is referred to as intonation. If you are expressive with your voice, you'll notice that you almost sing as you speak, with a lot of vocal variety in your tone. The best way to hold attention with your voice is to add energy to your delivery. Let your real emotions shine through and echo in your voice.

The ups and downs in tone not only add emphasis and impact to your message but also make you sound friendly, approachable, interesting and entertaining. A monotone voice will not hold the attention of your listeners very long. This is even more important in online calls and teleconferences.

Intonation tips

- Read a passage that has little meaning to you – something like a dictionary or a catalogue. Regardless of what you are reading, try to add emotion to your voice. Record yourself. Can you hear the difference between your 'angry voice' and your 'sad voice'? Does your 'boring voice' sound the same as your 'happy voice'?
- Read a short passage from an article or book. Place extra emphasis on words you feel are important. What happens to your intonation?

Resonance

The amount and location of the vibration of your voice is referred to as resonance. The vibration of your vocal folds is only one small part of the quality of your voice. What really determines how your voice sounds are the cavities in which it vibrates, such as your chest, throat, mouth and nose. The more open and relaxed these cavities are, the greater the resonance and the stronger the voice. When you are anxious, nervous or tense, your body tightens. In turn, the strength of your voice suffers because your voice can't resonate properly. You have trouble projecting your voice and end up sounding exactly the way you feel – weak, stressed and tense.

Resonance tips

- Relax.
- Make sure you have enough air and push that air through your vocal tract with the strength of your diaphragm.

From boring to brilliant

A great speaker is someone the audience enjoys listening to. They are passionate. Their voice is captivating. They don't just focus on language but have also perfected their use of paralanguage.

Drop the monotone 'corporate' voice that you think signals confidence and power, and start adding passion and energy to your delivery. Where language might fail because a listener doesn't always understand all the words, paralanguage will succeed in making your listener *feel* something. And that's what we know people remember – how you made them feel.

We can supercharge the feeling and passion in our messages by combining our language and paralanguage to emphasize important words in our messages. Consider this sentence: 'I didn't say he's my friend.' This sentence can imply six different meanings depending on the word you choose to emphasize. If you deliver the sentence in monotone with even stress on each word, we only get the meaning of the words. If you emphasize 'didn't', suddenly you're defensive. Emphasize 'he's', and now we wonder who you meant to talk about. Emphasize 'friend', and now you've got us focused on the type of relationship you have with this person.

In linguistics, this is called contrastive stress. We add impact and meaning to our words by applying vocal cues. We emphasize words by saying them louder and stretching them out longer. Our pitch rises and we use larger facial expressions to further support our meaning.

If you also add variation to your volume and tempo as you deliver your messages, you can really go from boring to brilliant in not only your formal presentations but also casual interactions.

Using a microphone

Now that so much of our communication has moved online to video calls, teleconferences and audio-only social media apps, our voices are constantly being heard through technology as we speak into microphones. Microphones (and Internet connections) can significantly change the quality and clarity of our voices.

Ask any video producer and they will tell you that although they specialize in making the picture look just right, the audio is the most important. Many of us know this intuitively. It's hard to stay focused on a video if the audio quality is poor.

Worse, poor audio quality could even affect the degree to which listeners trust you and your message. Researchers at the University of Southern California found that when people watched videos with poor and disrupted audio quality, they distrusted the message and the messenger more than those who watched the same video with good audio.[4]

Here are some basic tips for working with microphones in your online communication:

- The microphone reduces the need for you to project your voice. Be careful that you aren't shouting into your mic.
- If you have an external microphone attached to your computer, remember to choose that microphone in your computer settings (if the computer didn't recognize it automatically) as well as in your video-conferencing platform settings.
- Don't put the microphone too close to your mouth. You run the risk of 'popping' in the mic. This happens when you make a sound like 'P' and a quick burst of air hits the microphone. If the microphone is too close, your breath might also be picked up.
- If you are using a more professional microphone on a boom arm or standing on your desk, use a pop filter or speak into the mic at a 45-degree angle to avoid popping and hissing sounds.
- If you are using a headset microphone, typically used for a mobile phone, and the mic is dangling on the wire, you might need to move it closer to your mouth to get better sound quality. Make sure you don't cover your mouth for this, and be careful that the mic doesn't rub on your clothing.
- The built-in microphone on your computer is never good enough. It will pick up the buzz of your room, your computer fan and other noise, and can make you sound like you're in an echo chamber.
- In larger groups, stay muted when you aren't speaking. Having multiple live microphones can lead to disruptions in the sound quality of the call.

You might not have Siri's mellifluous voice, but the importance of using your voice well in our digital world is undeniable. If you are uncomfortable with the sound of your voice, of course there are coaches you can work with to change it. But unless you have habits that are dangerous to your vocal folds (for example, the increasingly common vocal fry that forces the voice into the lowest registers), I'd encourage you to embrace your authentic voice. Like your accent, it says a lot about you, serving as your unique vocal fingerprint.

Press UNMUTE

- Your voice is your most powerful tool of connection. Vary vocal cues such as pitch, volume, tempo, intonation and resonance so that you express emotion and connect with your listener.
- Use your voice to emphasize important words and phrases and add meaning to your message.
- Invest in a good microphone headset for your virtual calls and meetings. Good sound quality won't only hold your audience's attention, it will also make them trust you more.

9

🎙 Bad English – good for business

'My grammar? No one cares about my grammar!
As long as they can understand me, it's good enough.'[1]

'I'm sorry, what?'

We were nearing the end of our first consultation when, after noticing some common grammatical errors, I asked my new client, the Vice President for Greater Asia for an American multinational company, whether he'd be interested in reviewing his grammar as well. His response was far from what I expected.

I knew he was hiring me to help him with his presentation skills and to ensure his pronunciation was intelligible to the American Board of Directors, but why would he not want some help with his grammar at the same time?

After our meeting, I spent a lot of time thinking about his comments. Typically, people came to me (or were sent to me by their bosses or HR departments) so that I could 'fix' what is generally considered to be their poor English. Singapore even has a national 'Speak Good English' campaign that was at its peak when we had this conversation over a decade ago (and still exists today). Despite all that, here was a successful global leader (in an American company, no less) making me question whether bad English was really so bad after all.

How poor was his English, really? How much did it matter when he told me the global CEO 'do' a lot of conference calls? Did I misunderstand when he said his chief of staff 'make' his presentations, or even when he dropped the final 't' on words like 'collect' or 'contract'? A standard global English exam would have penalized him for these basic errors.

But I understood everything he said. Whether the grammar and pronunciation were what I considered to be 'correct' had no impact on our mutual understanding.

This is not to say that basic grammar, vocabulary and pronunciation are not important. We need a strong linguistic foundation in any language in order to communicate. In the case of this client, however, there was an invisible line at some point where the language was 'good enough' that his expertise (and confidence in his expertise) began to outweigh what I perceived as shortcomings in his expression of it.

As I battled the discomfort that most of us feel when confronted with an unconscious bias, I was a bit slow to realize that 'Isn't that the way it *should* be?' Wouldn't it be better if we were listened to and respected for our ideas regardless of how they are expressed?

Even though this made sense to me, I had hundreds of clients who were living proof that this was not the case in global business. A decade later and those numbers are in the thousands. I have built a business based on the clear fact that linguistic perfection combined with a strong dose of eloquence *does* matter to listeners at a deep, subconscious level.

But I continue to battle with the question: '*Should* it matter?' Who am I to decide what is right or wrong, good or bad? Is UK English more correct than US English? Is US English more proper than Singapore English? Who makes the rules? Who decides?

This became a real awakening for me. Isn't it time to redefine 'good' and 'bad' when it comes to language? How can a person's English be 'bad' if I can understand the meaning of their message? Isn't that the point? Surely, we should focus on the end result: clear, intelligible communication for the context and situation. As I encourage these 'bad' English speakers in the closing of my 2018 TEDx Talk on this subject, 'If you can understand, and you are being understood, then you speak "bad" English perfectly.'[2]

I believe that if we release this need for linguistic *perfection* and instead focus on *connection*, 'bad' English can actually be very good for business. Far from being 'bad' or 'less than', the way we use English in global settings is perfectly suited to increase mutual understanding across cultures and languages. It can play a pivotal role in helping you unmute yourself and your organization.

Who owns the English language?

It's difficult to estimate how many people in the world speak English because there is no official global data that charts language use. David Crystal, the author of over 100 books on the English language and linguistics, suggested in a 2008 article that there could be as many as two billion English speakers worldwide.[3]

Over a decade later, I feel we can accept this number as more than just a suggestion. Taking population growth into consideration in a country like India, and the growth of the English language industry in China, we can easily assume that at least one third of the world now speaks some level of English.

When we consider that there are only around 400–500 million native speakers of English,[4] it's hard to claim that any one variety of 'native' English is a 'standard'. Even the definitions and use of the terms 'native' and 'non-native' are questionable when it comes to using English as a global lingua franca (common language).

English native speakers in the West have long claimed ownership of the language. We are, of course, the ones who introduced the world to English through our conquering, colonizing and missionary efforts. We speak the language naturally and fluently as a birthright, and we benefit from that privilege throughout the world. We maintain an element of power over other language speakers when we can correct their grammar mistakes and point out a 'heavy accent' or 'poor pronunciation'.

The paradox lies in the fact that, in global communication, native speakers are actually the ones causing the problems. Many language specialists agree that native speakers can be harder to understand in global settings.[5] When English native speakers are outnumbered at least four to one, the English used in global settings is nothing like the English being taught in textbooks.

No one *owns* the English language. No one owns any language. Languages are living, breathing organisms that are constantly changing at the hands (and mouths) of their users. When you really understand the truth of this statement, you may notice that your relationship with the English language changes.

As typical English native speakers, who are often monolingual, we need to take more responsibility for our communication. We can no longer assume that we are masters of the language and that others need to speak to a standard easy for us to understand. We need to be open to the many variations of English that are spoken in the world and consider them equal to our own. We need to make a real effort to understand English in all its forms (even regional variations in our own countries) without judgement.

Let's look at the other side of the coin. For what is now close to two billion English users who learned the language in a classroom, the perspective needs to change as well. There is no reason to view Western English speakers as gatekeepers of the language.

There is no 'model' accent or variety of English. Assuming your foundations in English are strong enough that you are understood by others, the way we all speak the language is equally valid.

Is bad English good for business?

In an interview with Fredrik Härén for his book, *One World One Company*, Leif Johansson, the former CEO of Volvo Group, joked that their global, corporate language was 'bad English'.[6]

This definitely wasn't considered a disadvantage. In fact, 'bad' English allowed for greater idea generation and expression because there was no pressure to be perfect. Regardless of your language capabilities, your message would still be heard.

Embracing connection instead of perfection in the global workplace can be very good for global business. Here are just five reasons why.

Inclusivity

By embracing 'bad' English, you can give everyone a voice. Even those who aren't confident in their English skills can speak up and share their ideas, because they don't need to be afraid to make mistakes.

If they don't feel pressured by the company or their colleagues to be perfect, and they know that there won't be repercussions for small grammar mistakes in an internal report or slide deck, you will probably hear from a lot more people. This leads to greater idea generation and innovation as well as a sense of team belonging.

When everyone is able to contribute to the success of the company and they feel like their ideas are heard, you create a more innovative and collaborative workplace that has a positive impact on the company's bottom line.

Clarity

Speaking 'bad' English forces us to simplify our ideas to the very core and express them clearly, in language everyone can understand. Some people wrongly think of this as 'dumbing down' a topic.

As Albert Einstein apparently once said, 'If you can't explain it simply, you don't understand it well enough.' By removing jargon, idioms, slang and advanced vocabulary, we can ensure we get our point across the first time and have fewer misunderstandings. We'll take a closer look at exactly how to do this in Chapter 10.

Efficiency

For most people, it takes significantly longer to write something perfectly in a foreign language. The process includes a reliance on Google translate, second-guessing themselves and asking for colleagues' opinions before they can get it just right.

If you speak a foreign language, compare the time it takes to write an email in your native language versus the foreign language. Multiply the difference by the number of emails you write each day. You'll quickly see how a quest for perfection could end up costing you a large chunk of your workday.

In speaking situations, expression anxiety can be heightened when communicating in an additional language. This could result in people not speaking up at all or not being able to present their ideas as clearly as they'd like. If we reduce the need for perfection, we can increase people's comfort in communicating in English, and this can also increase their ability to do it well.

Agility

English has become the world's language. When your organization speaks English, you have many more opportunities available to you. You can quickly change the direction of the company, expand into other markets, acquire other entities or recruit global talent. You can move faster without as much need for translators and interpreters.

You also have greater knowledge sharing among your teams all over the world when they speak the same language and can learn from each other. English allows the company to respond and react to global forces with greater agility.

Fairness

Have you ever heard an eloquent speaker say absolutely nothing of real substance, yet still mesmerize their audience? It's amazing how impressive people can sound when using tone, pace and pause effectively, even though they have very little to say.

Most people believe unconsciously that eloquence and good ideas are connected. Great speakers can easily sway an audience to follow them, whether they have good, honest, moral ideas or not. We forget that some of the most infamous leaders, such as Hitler, Mussolini and Stalin, were also considered to be powerful, eloquent orators.

Great thinking is not a prerequisite for eloquence in any language. We unconsciously give more attention (and more promotions) to people who speak well, sometimes overlooking a lack of actual action or results. When we start listening to *what* people say instead of *how* they say it, the most talented people with the best ideas can start to rise to the top.

This is easier said than done. You need to consciously override your unconscious biases, which means you need to be aware of the unconscious biases that influence you. Are you giving preference to certain nationalities, accents, languages, skin colours, genders, ages, or anything else? Focus on the content only – not all the external factors. You can turn back to Chapter 2 and look at the Wheel of Culture (see page 17) for a selection of filters that could be influencing you.

Beyond bad English

My youngest daughter, Stella, was eight years old when she made a good friend at school from Korea. Soee didn't speak a word of English, but they talked and played together all day, every day. One day I got a call from Soee's mother. She was grateful that Stella had been so welcoming, especially when Soee couldn't speak English and the girls couldn't communicate.

I related this story to Stella, commending her on being such a good friend. She looked at me blankly and said, 'Why does she need to speak English? We can build sandcastles without talking about it.' What sandcastles could you build if you let go of a need for perfection and focused on connection instead?

Press UNMUTE

- View English as a tool to connect instead of a symbol of identity or source of power.
- Listen to the meaning of the message, not how it is communicated.
- Focus on connection, not perfection.

10

🎤 Understand and be understood

'You talk funny.'

'What do you mean, I "talk funny"?' I snapped back at my childhood friend, Nyrene.

'I don't know. It's weird. You sound different. Why are you talking like that?'

It took a while to understand what Nyrene meant. It was my first Christmas back in California after moving to Denmark in mid-2002. I couldn't imagine I had changed so much that I sounded foreign to her. It was hard for her to point out what was wrong. We finally deciphered the problem when we were wandering through the aisles of a bookstore and I pointed to a book, 'Hey, have you read this?'

'There! You just did it! We don't say it like that!'

She repeated my words, exaggerating my tone and lifting the pitch on 'read': 'Have you *read* this?'

I was still confused. She clarified: 'We say, "Have you read *this*?"' with an overexaggerated rising tone at the end of the question.

It took me a second to understand what was going on. At the time I was learning Danish and was having trouble feeling the intonation patterns. I came up with the idea to speak English (mostly in my head) with Danish intonation so I could start to 'feel' the language. I guess it had worked a little better than planned, because what Nyrene heard was me using a Danish intonation pattern on top of my English.

Once I realized what I was doing, I managed to switch back and started speaking 'normally' again. But I've noticed that every time I go back to the US, I sound more and more unlike the people around me, and I need to work harder and harder to sound 'normal' to them. After over 20 years of living in international environments, I have naturally changed the way I speak. Most of the changes happened subconsciously. Some were conscious decisions. All were with the intention of being best understood by everyone everywhere. It's in our interest to learn how to communicate as clearly as possible. By adapting our speech in subtle but powerful ways, we can be understood on the first try, every time. You might think that native speakers have an advantage and are easily understood, but we know that native speakers can be some of the most difficult to understand in international settings due to relaxed speech patterns, idioms and colloquialisms.

In a world that is increasingly global and interconnected, you don't even need to leave your living room to chat with colleagues, vendors or friends on the other side of the world. If we all make an effort to speak clearly and listen consciously, we can build stronger, more efficient teams that focus on inclusion and understanding.

Every conversation is a negotiation

On the global stage, every conversation is a new negotiation of meaning depending on who is speaking, who is listening and the context in which they are speaking. What is considered correct and understandable English spoken by an Indonesian and a Korean in their company headquarters in Germany will be very different from a conversation between a Canadian and an Australian in Singapore, or a Brit and a Frenchman in Paris.

What skills do we need to develop to prepare us for communication everywhere with everyone? First, we need to consider the language we use based on our context (or a lack thereof). Then we need to use verbal and non-verbal communication methods to best relay our messages clearly.

This is true regardless of your first language. I want to move away from the dichotomy of 'native' and 'non-native' speaker labels because, as we discussed in the last chapter, they shouldn't matter. We all come to global interactions as foreigners, so we all need to take responsibility for our communication in global settings. Let's take a closer look at how we can communicate with greater clarity and confidence.

Language and context

Global interactions lack the cultural context that is typically tied to individual varieties of English. Idioms, slang and jargon should be removed (or explicitly explained), because we don't share a common context for understanding. The English language is a tool in global business, not a cultural marker, and we can't expect people from other backgrounds to understand our local (or learned) slang and colloquialisms.

Many people and organizations have tried to develop global codes for using English. The UK's Plain English Campaign has been 'fighting for crystal-clear communication since 1979'.[1] They focus on the written word and award their Crystal Mark for documents that meet their standards of clarity.[2]

Others have attempted to create a simplified vocabulary that can be used among mixed levels of English speakers. Most notably, Voice of America (VOA) first published their Special English Word Book in 1962.[3] Now known as their Learning English programme, VOA broadcasts English language news and information through radio, satellite and the Internet throughout the world to international speakers of English. The Special English Word Book limits the vocabulary of these programmes to a set of 1,500 commonly used words.

Jean-Paul Nerrière attempted something similar in his creation of Globish, a controlled version of English that he suggests should be used in international settings. He published his 'Elements of Globish' in his 2009 ebook (co-authored by David Hon), *Globish the World Over*.[4] This subset of English is based on research Nerrière did during his work as Vice President for Europe, Middle East and Africa (EMEA) and, later, Vice President of International Marketing for IBM. His Globish language is based on a foundation of 1,500 words, plus up to 5,000 'children' (derivatives of the original 1,500 words).

I have a problem imposing strict limits to English vocabulary in global settings. We all have many ways of explaining ourselves, and I believe we can make ourselves clear with some effort on the part of both the speaker and the listener. Still, if we want to be best understood, we need some awareness of the areas of language that can cause confusion.

If we choose to use these speech elements, we must be prepared to explain ourselves, check for understanding, and clarify our meaning:

- Idioms (e.g. my hands are tied, go down the drain, red tape, smooth sailing, think outside the box, the elephant in the room)
- Phrasal verbs (e.g. run up against, run out of, run into, run over, run up, run for)
- Sports metaphors (e.g. three strikes, touchdown, touch base, slam dunk, pass the baton)
- Slang
- Abbreviations and acronyms
- Technical jargon
- Advanced, ornamental vocabulary

After living abroad for some time, I can remember a period when I mourned my English vocabulary, as I found it harder and harder to remember and use words that I typically would have dropped into educated conversation (partly for the sake of meaning and partly to impress). I had no need for them when conversing in global settings. Simpler words got my message across more easily.

While you don't need to fully remove these elements, be prepared to explain them in order to foster greater understanding. The explanations can add a lot of fun to the conversation and give an insight into another culture.

A problem arises when people assume a shared understanding of words and phrases that are not universally used. They sprinkle them in conversation and don't realize that their message is lost on their listeners. Your listener won't always ask for clarification, especially in a mixed work group or in front of their boss.

Accent bias

Our fast-thinking brains judge and categorize people the minute they open their mouths. In fact, we can detect a foreign accent in as little as 30 milliseconds.[5] If others sound different or are hard to understand, we put them in an 'other' and, usually, 'less than' category. It is then easier to discount what they say or to be inattentive. We place the blame on them for not speaking in a way that's easy for us to listen to.

When our brain strains to understand a variety of our language that we aren't used to hearing, it gets tired. Our brains are, by nature, quite lazy and they are always trying to reduce cognitive load. When someone is hard to understand, we risk 'switching off' and not paying as close attention. This has been shown to have serious ramifications for a person who sounds different. It can negatively impact entrepreneurs who are trying to get funding[6] or interviewees looking for higher-status jobs or customer-facing positions.[7]

I'm confident that the great majority of hiring managers are not consciously making these discriminatory decisions, and they would be shocked to see their own statistics. A mixture of perception (see Chapter 2) and fatigue combine to subconsciously influence people to make poor decisions. This is why it's so important to be conscious of language privilege and linguistic bias.

This is not only the case in global settings using English, but among native-speaking communities of every language. Regardless of the language, your brain will jump to conclusions about where a person is from, their education level, social status and even their race. This is where microaggressions can so easily show up in the workplace, such as, 'You didn't sound black on the phone.'[8]

We all have accents. Every time I say that someone will respond with, 'I think mine is pretty neutral.' No. It's only neutral to you and other people who sound just like you.

Just as there is no 'standard' English, there are no 'neutral' accents. You have an accent just like everyone else, and it will not sound 'neutral' to everyone. We all must work on the clarity of our speech so that we can be understood, and this has nothing to do with our accents.

Understanding

Instead of focusing on accents, it's more important to focus on clarity and understanding.

There is a long history of linguists trying to determine a core system of sounds in English that can ensure intelligibility across different varieties of English. As early as 1958, linguist Charles Francis Hockett proposed a common core of sounds.[9] Thirty years later, in 1989, the phonetician Bryan Jenner took this research further and outlined his Common Core: a list of ten mutually intelligible, common features of English pronunciation across native varieties (and a bonus mention regarding voice quality).[10] Both Hockett and Jenner were focused on developing a core that spanned their selection of native varieties of English.

Another decade later, in 2000, linguist Jennifer Jenkins published what would become a monumental work in the field of English pronunciation: *The Phonology of English as an International Language*.[11] In it she proposed her Lingua Franca Core (LFC), which focused on the speech elements that needed to be in place for international speakers of English to understand each other. Instead of trying to sound like the Queen, learners could now focus on being intelligible instead of 'reducing' their accents.[12]

Although this core was designed to be used for international English speakers so they could best understand each other, I've found that understanding the LFC and applying it to my own speech has helped me to be better understood in my global relationships. Here are just a few ways you might adapt your speech in global settings:

- Articulate consonant sounds. Every consonant should sound unique.
- Letters 'R' and 'T' are especially important and should always be clearly pronounced.
- Use a consistent set of vowel sounds (don't mix between US and UK or regional varieties, for example).
- Pay attention to the vowel sound in words like 'girl', 'curl' and 'shirt'. That is the only vowel sound that sounds the same across accents.
- Group longer sentences into smaller chunks and take more pauses. This will also help you to slow down.
- Emphasize the most meaningful words.

Beyond language

In your focus on clear speech and choosing the best words, don't forget the communication skills that go far beyond language. You can create or enhance your meaning through every gesture, the tone of your voice and the energy you bring to a conversation. Use a consistent pace, speak slower than usual, and pause often to help others understand you. Listen with care (as outlined in Chapter 4), give visual and vocal feedback where necessary and ask for clarification when needed.

As much as I love image-heavy presentation slides with very little text, in some settings, text helps to make your visuals more inclusive. By adding text explanations to your slides, you help those who might have trouble understanding you or following the pace of your presentation. If you need to use words that are difficult for you to pronounce, write them on your slide, so your audience will make the connection between what they see and what they hear.

Checking for understanding

If you think that asking 'Does everyone understand?' or 'Any questions?' is a good check for understanding, you'll be surprised. You will likely be in situations where people are not comfortable telling you they don't understand. They might feel embarrassed to ask questions or to speak up. This could be due to language issues, culture or power structures in the company. Newer employees find it very difficult to ask a superior for clarification, thinking that it will negatively reflect on them.

A better check would be to ask others to summarize or rephrase what has been said, for example:

- 'What actions are you taking now, after this meeting?'
- 'Can you summarize the main points of the meeting for us?'
- 'Can you explain your understanding of this to me?'
- 'What does this chart mean to you?'

Follow up meetings with detailed minutes so people can refer back to conversations they might not have fully understood. We can never be too clear in global settings.

Asking for clarification

Conversely, you will also be in situations where you'll need to make sure you've understood correctly. Here are some ways you might ask for clarification:

- Ask the speaker to rephrase (not repeat) what they just said. If you didn't understand the first time, you probably won't understand it the second time!
- Ask the speaker to spell or to write the words on a white board (real or virtual). Putting communication in writing can often help to clarify important points.

Accent recognition

Another great way to improve global understanding (and become a more conscious listener, as we discussed in Chapter 4) is to get more familiar with accented varieties of English. Listen to English talk radio from different parts of the world, watch or listen to TED or TEDx Talks or join audio-based social networks that allow you to have authentic conversations with people all over the world.

The more contact you have with speakers with a specific accent, the easier they will be to understand. If you know you need to communicate with people from one language family, let's say German, then learn about the sounds in German and why German speakers typically pronounce words certain ways.

This kind of training can teach you the basic codes of accented English and open up a whole new world of understanding.

Press UNMUTE

- Choose your words carefully and avoid culturally charged idioms and metaphors.
- Articulate clearly, paying attention to areas of your own accent that could cause confusion.
- Slow down, speak up and check for understanding often.
- Use non-verbal communication to help make yourself clear.
- Familiarize yourself with all kinds of accented English so you can better understand others.

🎙 PART III:
INSPIRE ACTION

Connected Communication

🎙 The key to happiness

'Good relationships keep us happier and healthier. Period.'[1]

This is how Robert Waldinger summarizes the findings of over 80 years of research in the Harvard Study of Adult Development. He is the fourth director of this study that has tracked the lives of 724 men, starting from their late teenage years, and now continues to study 1,300 of their children.

The study didn't set out to look so closely at relationships. The early researchers were focused on biological factors, such as skull measurements and organ function, to discover the physical attributes that might lead to a longer life. As the participants got older, an astute researcher noticed that the quality of relationships had the strongest correlation to longevity. They also found that loneliness could be as toxic and detrimental to lifespan as smoking and drinking in excess.[2]

Humans are social animals. We are born with an innate need for human connection. Without it, we become lonely and depressed, and it can significantly affect our quality of life. This is also true in the workplace. Of the 2,141 people surveyed by the Institute of Leadership and Management in January 2020, 77 per cent thought that good relationships were essential for job satisfaction. This puts relationships at the very top of the list of factors influencing job satisfaction.[3]

Having a few close relationships at work has also been shown to reduce stress and burnout while increasing efficiency, productivity and overall engagement.[4] This is more important than ever when, at the time of writing, we stand on the brink of what many are referring to as a 'Great Resignation'. Microsoft's Work Trend Index reports that 41 per cent of employees planned to leave their jobs in 2021.[5] Developing an unmuted culture where relationships are in focus will be essential for organizations to survive in our new world of work.

As we will see in Chapter 12, we can measure the strength of connections at work and identify the most connected members of our teams. If we lose these 'influencers', there is a 500 per cent greater chance that the people they have direct relationships with will also leave the company within six months.[6] The importance of our relationships in an organization cannot be overlooked.

I think we all know this to be true intuitively, but what's harder to figure out is how to build trusting, respectful relationships. It's difficult enough in our personal lives but doing it in the workplace brings additional challenges. Still, it's only through strong relationships that we can build an unmuted culture of conscious and confident communication. Our connections are the most important part of the equation. The stronger they are, the more comfortable we feel sharing our ideas and speaking up in the organization.

Everyone is *able* to build relationships with others. We're born with this ability in our DNA. The real question is whether we are *willing*. Relationships are something that we choose, and that choice does not come without risk. Relationships require us to take risks with our emotions and, especially in the workplace, emotions are something we usually try to avoid.

This is changing. If we have learned anything during the COVID-19 pandemic, it is that leaders need to develop their emotional awareness and build personal relationships with their people. Often, we think of this as being outside the scope of the job description. Work comes first, building relationships second or should only be addressed in our 'free time'. This couldn't be more backwards. You won't get the work done unless you have strong relationships with those around you *first*.

Emotional contagion

Our emotions are incredibly powerful. We feel them in a very physical way, and there is significant evidence to suggest that these feelings cross cultures and languages. We have universal physical sensations that are tied to different feelings (e.g. a racing heart, tension in the face, stiffness in limbs, etc.).[7]

We feel emotions, and not just our own. They are contagious; hence the term 'emotional contagion'. We have a natural tendency to mimic those around us and pick up on their feelings. When you see other people display emotion, you will have a natural tendency to copy them. You likely won't know this is happening, and it can be as subtle as a slight curl of the lips when you see someone smile or a tightening of the eyes if someone is scowling. You might hear people comment on someone's 'energy' or 'mood' and how they like or don't like to be around them. There are probably certain people you know who have a lot of 'charisma' or 'presence'. You feel them when they enter a room. Their emotional messaging (in their body language, tone of voice, facial expressions or words) is very clear. If you are in a more neutral emotional state, their feelings will transfer to you, and you could end up leaving feeling just as happy (or as anxious) as them.

Imagine how quickly one rotten apple can spoil the bunch. At the same time, someone with a positive outlook and emotional state can sway a group in a more positive direction. It's important to understand your own and others' emotions so you can better manage the emotional contagion that you might feel.

Emotional contagion can be used in your favour both within the company and with external clients and stakeholders. For example, people who harness positive emotions when interacting with clients and customers can help an aggressive complainer leave in a happier state.

If you can identify your own emotions, feel the emotions of others and manage your emotional responses in certain situations, then you exhibit high levels of emotional intelligence. Daniel Goleman popularized the concept of emotional intelligence just over 25 years ago in his book *Emotional Intelligence: Why It Can Matter More Than IQ.*[8] Since then, hundreds of studies have shown how emotional intelligence (EQ) *does* matter more than IQ, and that IQ is not a valid predictor of life success.

Building unmuted relationships

The most important element in unmuted relationships is trust.

Our world is facing a serious trust deficit. The 2021 Edelman Trust Barometer delivers shocking statistics about our current trust of government, business, NGOs and the media. We have more information than ever before, but no one knows what they can believe. This is why Edelman named 2021 the year we declared 'information bankruptcy'.[9] This is a serious crisis that can and will affect our social and economic recoveries globally.

Trust in our governments is at an all-time low, while business is the only institution that is viewed as both competent and ethical. I'd hardly call this a big win, as it's basically an award for 'best of the worst'. Business received a trust score of 61 out of 100. CEOs are also more mistrusted than ever before, even though 86 per cent of respondents expect CEOs to speak out on social challenges. What are we to do?

The Edelman report measures trust along two dimensions: competence and ethics. This is in keeping with how we judge trust in our relationships. I like to refer to these dimensions as brain trust and heart trust, respectively.

Brain trust

Do I think this person knows what they are talking about? Do I trust this person to do their research? Can I consistently count on this person to get the job done?

Table 11.1 The Trust Quadrant

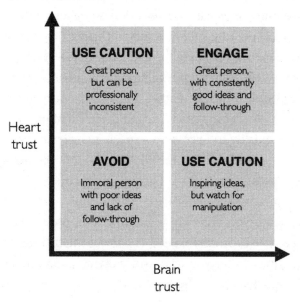

You build brain trust with people by consistently showing up, sharing ideas and getting the job done. You show integrity, check your sources, dig deep and communicate your thoughts clearly and concisely. You don't always have to be right and, in fact, you're the first to admit when you're wrong. You make mistakes and are honest about them. You can expect the same consistent behaviours from the other person as well.

Heart trust

Do I feel a connection to this person? If I am vulnerable, will this person take advantage of me? Does this person treat others fairly? Do I trust the intentions in their heart?

You are emotionally intelligent and understand the motivations of those around you. You are authentic and vulnerable and disclose information about yourself. You are a conscious and caring communicator. We form trusting bonds when we share our feelings with others and disclose information about ourselves. You must trust others first if you want them to trust you.

When you build both brain and heart trust, you will have the strongest connection of all. Not only do you believe you can count on the person to show integrity and follow through, you also know you can count on them to be there for you emotionally if needed.

At the opposite extreme, if you fail to build brain or heart trust, it will be close to impossible to work together unless under special circumstances (i.e. a crisis or emergency situation). In these situations you are forced to build trust quickly to overcome a specific challenge. Sometimes this quick trust can grow based on the bonding that occurs during crisis.

One last type of trust that has become more common in remote and hybrid workplaces is passable trust. This is when you choose to trust someone, even if you don't know them well, in order to accomplish a common goal or project. Passable trust will often transition to heart and/or brain trust after you have worked with the same person a few times and come to rely on them.

Empathy and understanding

Very few people have poor intentions and purposely try to hurt others. However, we are often quick to be offended, not because of what someone has said or done, but because of something the person sparked in us. Maybe their words or mannerisms reminded us of someone else we have had a bad experience with. Perhaps our assumptions of the world and that person coloured their remarks. Or maybe we jumped to conclusions about what they meant instead of really taking the time to listen.

If you are shocked or saddened by someone's opinion, comments or even a social media post, ask yourself if you could have misunderstood. Ask the person to clarify what they mean and really listen to their reply. Think about how and why they might see the world differently than you do. It takes a very conscious communicator (see Part I) to show real empathy and understanding. And just because you show empathy and understanding, does not mean that you must agree.

Having empathy also doesn't require you to be extra nice to everyone and never criticize or challenge. In her book, *Radical Candor*, Kim

Scott calls this 'ruinous empathy'.[10] Being constantly agreeable, or giving hollow praise just to be nice, will stunt the progress of a team and will be the quickest road to failure as a leader.

The hazards of toxic environments

It might be easy to assume that if no one is complaining, then everyone must be happy. Unfortunately, this is a very dangerous assumption. You might think that your team is full of work horses, independently crunching the numbers and hitting targets, but if your people don't talk to you, there is probably a problem. When confident and conscious communicators are stuck in a disconnected, toxic environment, they press mute. Here are some reasons for your team's silence:

- They have lost heart trust in you because you do not show integrity.
- They have lost brain trust in you because you disregard the group consensus and do things your way.
- They don't feel connected to you or the company vision.
- They fear that anything they say could negatively affect them and their role (e.g. a negative performance review, losing the next promotion or being fired).
- They feel overlooked and undervalued and that their ideas don't matter.
- They worry that their ideas really aren't good enough, so they stop voicing them.
- They fear personal attacks.

A safe and connected environment is key to a productive, high-performing team. We'll spend the rest of Part III taking a closer look at how we can create this.

Relationships and technology

As we move the great majority of our communication online, it might seem like we are more connected than ever before. But when it comes to our relationships, it is the quality of our connections that matters, not how easy it is for us to connect. Hyperconnectivity can have the opposite effect: overwhelming us with information through myriad communication channels, making it more difficult to cut through the noise and make decisions about who and what really matter to us.

Can we fulfil our human connection needs through technology the same way we do face-to-face interaction? Do we get the same feel-good vibes in a virtual meeting as we do a real one? Research is beginning to show that we don't. As Microsoft tracked workplace connection over the course of the pandemic, they made some interesting discoveries.[11] As we went into our first lockdowns throughout the world, people turned to their closest networks, friends and teammates for support. They were actually more connected with these people than normal during the first months of the pandemic.

This was at the cost of their wider networks. People drastically cut their interactions with people they weren't as close to. This led to silos forming in many organizations and leaders lamenting that they couldn't get cross-functional teams to connect. This could be a serious concern for dispersed teams over time if hybrid work continues (and every sign says it will). Microsoft researchers are optimistic, however. Looking to data from New Zealand, a country that was one of the first to resume a sense of normalcy, they could see that relationships rebounded once lockdowns ended.

Computer-mediated communication is the shining star when it comes to maintaining human connection from a distance. At the start of lockdowns and the shift to online work, every meeting turned into a video call. Extra meetings were arranged that never would have happened in the office, because it was so easy to set up a video call, especially with team members in other countries.

We were spending more hours in meetings than ever, and the video call became a very good substitute for face-to-face communication. Soon people started to complain of 'Zoom fatigue', the feeling of exhaustion after being forced to spend hours on camera 'on display' for their colleagues, clients, family and friends.

These video calls should have allowed us to make our interactions as close to face-to-face reality as possible by including non-verbal social cues, such as gestures and facial expressions, while also allowing us to hear each other's voices. So why didn't we feel as energized after these calls as some of us (the more extroverted ones, anyway) would have felt normally?

In one of the first studies to be carried out on the effects of computer-mediated communication during the pandemic, researchers found that the video call wasn't the most favoured mode of communication, and it didn't make us feel the most connected. Instead, it was our good, old-fashioned telephone.[12]

The researchers believe this could be due to the more relaxed nature of the telephone, where we aren't being watched. It also allows us to multitask and perform other tasks around the (home) office while speaking, which allows us to move around if we want to pace instead of being seated in front of a screen.[13] Combined with the research mentioned in Chapter 8, which found that we can identify emotion more accurately when there is no visual stimulus present, it's understandable that the majority of people started using their mobile phones for telephone calls again instead of just surfing social media.[14]

Speaking of social media, the same study found that this addictive distraction was, unsurprisingly, the most detrimental form of communication for our moods, leading to greater loneliness and stress. This was the case regardless of whether people were using it actively (posting their own content, sending messages to others) or passively (scrolling through other people's feeds).

When it comes to maintaining our current relationships and building new ones in the new remote workspace, less technology may be more. Imitating the face-to-face experience will not necessarily help people meet their social needs, and sometimes a phone call or email will do more to further your relationship than a video call.

Press UNMUTE

- If you want a long, healthy life, prioritize your relationships higher than your work. Engaging with the people who mean something to you is the highest form of self-care.
- Work on building your brain trust and your heart trust. Do you do your research and check your sources? Do you speak to be heard or because you have something important to say? Do you do what you say you'll do with the best intentions? Do an integrity check.
- Focus on emotions. Make people feel something with your communication.
- Show empathy and understanding and make relationship-building one of your core work activities.

🎙 We're all connected (or not)

'But how do I know who's doing great work for our company in other parts of the world?'

This question came from a global HR manager during a webinar I was conducting called 'Connected Leadership'. It surprised me but was great proof of the disconnection many global teams face. [1]

'Um... ask your colleagues in the other offices? You must communicate with HR in the other countries... right?' That seems to have been a very large assumption on my part.

I had just shared an all-too-common story about a multinational company that, during the pandemic, developed a fancy, online, internal training portal. They then asked all their leaders in the global headquarters based in Europe to run webinars on best practices. Leaders in the Asia and Pacific (APAC) office wondered why they weren't being asked to run these sessions, since they were the only ones turning a profit globally. What exactly was HQ going to teach them?

An initiative that was meant to bring the global company together in a time of crisis backfired horribly and left many of their most talented leaders across the world feeling overlooked, undervalued and disconnected.

How connected do you feel to your colleagues, your bosses or your team? This is a difficult and subjective question that could elicit all kinds of answers. How can we possibly measure connection? Even though you might have trouble putting numbers on your feelings, modern technology and big data can answer that question for you.

Researchers have been trying to map the strength of social networks and their connections since the 1960s. It was a long and tedious process to collect and analyze data back then, mostly done by hand.[2] Sixty years later and we can process enormous data sets around the clock and in real time. With an increasing shift to remote work and almost all our communication moving online, our digital data pools are growing at an exponential rate. There is little that companies don't know (or can't find out) about their people. But having data, analyzing data and applying data are all very different things.

Much of the data collected by newly formed People Analytics departments are simple demographics: gender, ethnicity, location, absenteeism, age, education, salary level, and so on. They can also collect and process the amount of time spent working and exactly how that time is spent by tracking computer and application use. This is all interesting data to gather. It can help in hiring decisions, measuring demographic diversity, identifying training gaps and finding performance potential. The problem is that the data only tells the company about the individuals. It doesn't tell them much about the relationships between individuals.

When we look around the office, these relationships are invisible. But by using relational analysis we can now map the entire organizational network or just individual departments or teams on paper. We can find out who the influencers are (hint: it's probably not anyone on the leadership team), who trusts whom, how teams are connected and whether there are divisions operating independently of each other, creating their own dangerous 'silos' and not sharing information. We can see the communication channels (or lack thereof) in black and white. Instead of guessing why there are communication breakdowns and misunderstandings, we can see the problems in the data.

The unmuted organization is built on a foundation of open, trusting connections that foster conscious and confident communication. The first step is to know what the current organizational network looks like. Not only is it fascinating to uncover this information, but it also offers tremendous opportunities to increase ideation, innovation and efficiency while decreasing possible vulnerabilities and communication bottlenecks.

There are two ways to collect relational data: passive and active. Passive data collection refers to the mining of employee data from their digital actions and interactions. Active data collection consists of sending employees surveys and questionnaires.

Passive data collection

The communication tools we use at work track every interaction and the content within those interactions. It could be an email, text message or even a time stamp when you log on to the company network. Every action you take within company networks, and even some outside of them, can be monitored, tracked and analyzed.

Passive collection of data happens automatically once a company has established a system for it and can be instantly analyzed to produce real-time data results. Companies trust passive data more than questionnaires or surveys because they capture real behaviour. Surveys are self-assessments and can be inaccurate. You might write on a survey that you have approximately seven interactions with John per day (because you've likely never paid attention to this before), but your email and internal messenger data show that you average 23 interactions. It's a bit like guessing how many hours you spend wasting time on your phone. You are probably shocked every time you check the screen-time data.

Interesting relational analysis can be done with communicative data like email correspondence. Some researchers use computational linguistics methods to analyze communication styles, shared vocabulary and alignment of values to determine how company culture influences thoughts, behaviours and relationships at work.[3] This is only the beginning when it comes to deciphering the language we use and what it means within the organization.

A caveat of passive data is that it only reveals the daily transactional interactions. It does not reveal serendipitous relationships that you lean on for innovation, complex problem-solving and change; for example, when you are faced with a problem and you know exactly who to call for help – someone you worked with five years ago in another company. Passive data misses these touchpoints.

It's important to be careful how passive data is collected, analyzed and managed in organizations that want to develop an unmuted culture. We'll talk about data security a little later, but it is worth mentioning now how important transparency and anonymity are in the handling of this data.

Active data collection

Henry Ward, the CEO of equity management firm Carta, wanted to uncover the invisible relationship networks – what he calls the 'shadow org chart' – of his then 250 employees across four offices. He engaged Innovisor, a global leader in organizational network analysis, to carry out active data collection in the form of a survey. They asked employees three simple questions tailored to his objective:

1) Who energizes you at work? (list four or more people)
2) Who do you go to for help and advice? (list four or more people)
3) Who do you go to when a decision needs to be made? (list four or more people)

From these simple questions they could connect nominators to nominees, thus creating a directional network map. Their algorithms then helped them to discover that just nine employees (non-managers) influenced 70 per cent of the organization, and if they expanded to second-tier connections, they could reach all 250 employees. As Henry Ward jokes, 'If we wanted to spread a meme, these are the nine that we'd start with.'[4]

Who's really running your organization?

Henry Ward had his suspicions confirmed that the traditional, hierarchical organizational chart is not a true representation of how people work together or relate to each other. We get a better picture of these working relationships when we look at the network map.

Over the last 15 years of collecting data, Innovisor has found that as little as 3 per cent of an organization, department or team can influence up to 90 per cent of the larger group in question. Even more interesting is that those 3 per cent very seldom sit among the top leadership of the organization.[5] Innovisor call this the '3% Rule'.

Knowing who the 3 per cent are is crucial, and Jeppe Vilstrup Hansgaard, CEO of Innovisor, says he hasn't yet seen the leadership of any company guess their top influencer correctly.[6] They tend to be people who don't have special attributes on the traditional organizational chart, but their connections within and outside the company make them pivotal to the company's success.

These individuals set the tone for the organization. If they are happy, everyone is happy. If they are upset or, even worse, if they quit, they could take the company down with them. Innovisor found that there is a 500 per cent higher chance that a direct connection of an influencer will follow that influencer out the door within six months. That's the power of strong relationships and human connection at work.[7]

In our world of social media and vanity metrics, it's important to note that influence is not defined by the largest number of connections. What's most important is aggregate prominence.[8] Aggregate prominence measures how well the influencer's connections are connected and, in turn, how well those connections are connected. You don't need to know everyone to have influence. You just need to know the *right* people.

Applying the data to develop an unmuted culture

Once you have mapped the informal networks of your organization, have a better understanding of your challenges and recognize your strengths, you'll find that your next steps to developing an unmuted organization become surprisingly clear.

Engage influencers

Set up informal meetings between leadership and influencers so leadership can stay aware of the informal conversations going on in the company. Get ideas and buy-in from influencers for big initiatives that will impact the larger organization. Shape internal communications based on input from influencers and include them in the dissemination of that information.

Finally, develop ways to motivate and enable your influencers within their teams.

Build bridges between silos

Create new work groups across silos. Design team-building activities, training courses or other events that initiate interaction across silos. This is actually easier to do in remote work environments. People who typically wouldn't have much to do with each other due to department divisions or office locations can be brought together more easily online.

Bring outliers into the group

Check the level of conscious communication in the team and consider cultural assessments to raise cultural intelligence. Make sure that outliers are placed in supportive teams that admire their special skills and abilities and respect their uniqueness.

Make up for vulnerabilities

Strengthen your networks by adding support where the network is vulnerable. For example, if two teams are only connected through one person, it's important to create more connections there. Organize leadership, human skills and communication training for areas of the network that show a need for better connection.

It looks good — why won't they speak up?

If the network map shows strong connections, but team members are having difficulty speaking up, check for skills gaps and supplement with training in communicative competencies and confidence. If there is still silence, check in with influencers to see if they know something you don't. Run a pulse survey to measure engagement levels. Find out if there is a bigger problem like a toxic manager who makes people fear speaking up.

Check the network map

Depending on the map of your organization, you could have any number of additional concerns. Having data to back up your decision-making process can give you and your teams the confidence to trust the process and initiate change.

After you have implemented changes to bring the organization closer together, run the analysis again to see how the network map has changed. Are outliers now included? Have silos broken down? The best part about organizational network analysis is that you can see hard results for soft-skill improvements.

Data ethics

In the 2018 Global Human Capital Trends survey published by Deloitte, 84 per cent of respondents thought people analytics were 'important' or 'very important', but only 10 per cent felt they were 'very ready' to handle the challenge of data security.[9]

Unmuted organizations are based on transparency and trust. It's difficult to speak openly and share information if you are always worried about how it might be used (or misused). It is absolutely essential that companies have documented policies concerning *which* data is being collected and *how* it is being collected and analyzed. Companies should also outline what the data is being used for, where it will be distributed and how it will be stored and protected. Any passive data collection of text messages, email content, calendar details, voice communications, social media, video calls or any other forms of communication must be fully anonymous.

Relational analytics tools can provide organizations with amazing opportunities, but the potential risks associated with a data breach could be devastating. With the newer General Data Protection Regulations (GDPR) in Europe, companies need to tighten their security and take data management very seriously.

There is a fine line between collecting anonymous data for useful purposes and becoming 'big brother'. If employees feel like they have no privacy or that there is no safe space to voice opinions, concerns or just be themselves, there will be no chance of developing an unmuted organization.

Press UNMUTE

- Map your organizational network to find your communication channels and influencers.
- Analyze your network map to find out which teams, departments, regions or individuals are on mute, and design programmes to rectify silos and roadblocks to communication.
- Publish a Data Ethics Policy for your company to clearly outline the data being collected and how it is collected, analyzed, shared, stored and protected.

🎙 Creating a safe environment

'DO NOT DISTURB. I'M SOCIAL DISTANCING.'
As seen on a T-shirt, 2020

I laughed when I saw an advertisement for this T-shirt, and I even considered buying one myself. The truth was, after living in crowded Singapore for over a decade, I was happy to finally have people stand one metre away from me in the supermarket. Singapore's social distance was my normal personal space.

Many people questioned the use of the term 'social distance' to describe the physical distance we experienced during the pandemic. Georg Simmel, the sociologist who first coined this term in the early 1900s would have been the most surprised by the T-shirt.[1] He used the term to refer to the degree of emotional or cognitive connection among those in a group.

The theory goes that the more we have in common with each other and feel we belong in a group, the better we will work together because there is less social distance. The goal is to minimize social distance and increase belonging in a team. Teams with high social distance have difficulty building empathy and understanding. This concept has been addressed in hundreds of studies relating to race, ethnicity and intercultural relationships, and it is cited as one of the largest hurdles to overcome in dispersed, multicultural teams.

Fast forward over 100 years, and suddenly the term 'social distance' has a very different meaning. It is something we should maximize (and also print on T-shirts).

But physical distance and social distance are two very different things. Just as we can be physically close to each other, but socially and psychologically far (consider a failing marriage or when you first move to a foreign country), the opposite can also be true. Some people reported feeling *more* connected with their closest network during the beginning of the pandemic, despite the physical distance created by lockdowns.[2]

Perhaps it was due to the shared human experience of lockdowns and loneliness, or maybe it was because we suddenly got to peek into our boss's living room and meet their pets. In any case, the dynamics of our working world were significantly changed.

Where these two examples of the term 'social distance' overlap is that they are both steeped in fear. In the sociological definition, fear is created when people in a group are wary of an outsider and don't allow them to fully participate in the group. Or the outsider worries they won't be accepted in the group or dreads embarrassment because they are different. Our modern use of 'social distance' comes from the fear of physical closeness and viral contagion.

It's this *fear* that needs to be addressed in the unmuted workplace. We must decrease the fear that is present with social distance (the sociological kind) so that we can increase feelings of social and psychological safety. This is easier said than done.

Reducing social distance

Harvard business school professor Tsedal Neeley has been studying global teams for almost two decades. Her SPLIT framework looks at a business's global Structure, Processes, Language, Identity and Technology to determine how a company can reduce social distance and operate as one.[3] It serves as an excellent framework through which one can apply many of the topics discussed in this book.

Structure

How does the physical structure of the business create or reduce social distance? Where are offices located? Do people work from home? Are there time zone considerations? The physical structure of the business will have an enormous effect on the communication systems of the company and how well connected (or disconnected) people feel.

Processes

Most of this book is focused on the interpersonal processes that are needed to build trust and connection in a workplace (whether dispersed or not): self-awareness, confidence, belonging, communication and strong relationships. The story in Chapter 12 about the European HQ excluding subject experts from their global locations in their learning platform is an example of overlooking the interpersonal relationships that are necessary in global business.

Language

Neeley is one of just a few global business researchers who I see highlighting the significant impact that language has on global business success. As outlined in Parts I and II, we cannot overlook the importance of a shared language and the advantages and disadvantages it presents for global teams.[4]

Identity

The issue of cross-cultural communication is an obvious challenge in global business. The lessons from Part I can help to tackle the problems of perception, stereotypes and assumptions based on location, age, gender, culture and many other factors.

Technology

In Chapter 15, we'll take a closer look at how technology can help us bridge the gaps of working from home, hybrid offices and global teams.

We have many tools at our disposal that can help us to decrease social distance within dispersed teams.

When you manage the SPLIT and decrease social distance, people have a stronger sense of belonging at work. More importantly, when social distance goes down, psychological safety goes up.

Introducing psychological safety

In 2012, Google researchers set out to identify the characteristics of a high-performing team. Their earlier research efforts in Project Oxygen, in which they studied the characteristics that make a good manager, had been hugely successful. Now it was time to turn their attention to their teams. Project Aristotle became a multi-year study of over 180 teams. It was set to prove that, as Aristotle himself said, 'The whole is greater than the sum of its parts.'

They drilled through all the research on what makes a team great. They compiled all the numbers and data they had in their People Analytics department. They couldn't find any patterns. It wasn't until they landed on research in the area of psychological safety that things finally started to click.[5]

Amy Edmondson made waves in the field of organizational psychology when her dissertation research on psychological safety was published in a leading academic journal in 1999.[6] Psychological safety refers to our ability to take an interpersonal risk by speaking up and being candid with others, without fearing negative retribution, punishment or humiliation. A psychologically safe environment is exactly what we need to help people feel comfortable pressing unmute.

When Google uncovered Edmondson's research, they started looking at their own data differently. They had been looking at the 'who' of their teams: background, skill sets, personalities. They realized they needed to look at the 'how'. How did these individuals come together and interact? How comfortable were they in their relationships? How open and candid were they in their communication? How productive were they in their conflicts?

Google found, in full support of Edmondson's research, that the most significant factor in team effectiveness was the level of psychological safety that leaders were able to foster within the team. There were other distinguishing factors, but safety underpinned everything. Without it, the other factors would be meaningless.[7]

Creating a psychologically safe environment

If we are to create a safe environment where people feel comfortable pressing unmute and sharing their ideas, there are some shifts that Edmondson suggests organizations need to make to company culture.

I'll focus here on the two most important ones needed in an unmuted workplace, which are very closely linked: reframing failure and developing a culture of curiosity and learning.

Reframing failure

Sara Blakely, the founder of Spanx, started her company with $5,000 in her pocket and a serious growth mindset. She persevered through two full years of hearing 'no' before she could finally get her idea off the ground. Blakely says this resilience is a gift from her father.

She has often told the story of how her dad would ask her and her brother at the dinner table, 'What did you fail at this week?' If they didn't have something to say, he would be disappointed. She says that growing up with this mindset reframed the concept of failure for her. When Blakely failed, her dad would give her a high five and say, 'Congratulations! Way to go!' They celebrated failure, because in their house the only true failure was not trying at all.[8]

Most people have a natural fear of failure. No one wants to feel embarrassed at work or be made to feel 'less than'. So if we want people to speak up, we must reframe what it means to fail. When employees are afraid of making mistakes, they won't be very willing to speak up, either with their own ideas or to report serious errors they find that could cost the company dearly.

People will always make mistakes. There is little we can do to prevent that. I like the way Edmondson defines three different types of failure that must be treated in different ways: preventable failure (due to human error), complex failure (due to a variety of complex and variable factors) and intelligent failure (due to experimentation and calculated risk).[9]

The key is to see all these types of failure as an opportunity to learn and grow. Preventable failure points to a gap in skill sets, which can be improved with training. The complex error might highlight a system problem, which offers an opportunity to take a closer look at risk factors and design more efficient systems. And intelligent failure should be celebrated. The only way for a company to come up with excellent products and solutions is to test ideas, run experiments and be creative. There won't always be a positive outcome, but there is a lot of learning in the process.

Developing a culture of curiosity and learning

This concept of learning is pivotal to creating teams of people who willingly unmute. Every conversation must be seen as an opportunity to learn. Even the boss can learn something when team members are given the freedom, opportunity and space to share their ideas.

A learning culture, by nature, requires the humility of its members. Anyone who thinks they know all the answers will never learn anything. This is especially true if leaders hold on to the power associated with 'knowing it all'. Only the humble leader will be able to create the learning environment necessary to help team members open up.

Both Google and Edmondson found great variation in levels of psychological safety across teams. Some teams are high-performing and safe, while others stagnate. This usually comes down to the interpersonal skills of the leader. Complex human skills are needed to run a safe, efficient and unmuted team. We'll take a closer look at many of these in Chapter 14. Developing psychological safety in teams is not a quick fix or a one-off process, but rather a long-term goal that needs to be worked on consistently.

Psychological safety in dispersed teams

The original concept of social distance didn't only apply to the *feeling* of distance between two people. It also took into consideration the physical distance present. One of the ways we are able to decrease social distance is by creating context. We do this most easily when we occupy the same space, whether that's working in an office, chatting in a restaurant or living together in a home.

This is the most obvious challenge that dispersed teams need to manage. Most of the informal bonding and trust-building in a workplace happens during spontaneous interactions: bumping into each other in the pantry while refilling coffee, passing each other in the halls and stopping for a chat or overhearing a phone conversation and passing someone the file they need in that moment. These short, spontaneous interactions are desperately missed in teams that work remotely.

It sounds paradoxical, but we need to start scheduling spontaneous interaction. It's not the interaction itself that needs to be entered into the calendar. The important issue is creating the space for the interaction: five minutes set aside at the beginning of a meeting for small talk and catching up, or scheduling time to call colleagues and direct reports just to check in and see how things are going. These are simple ways to stay connected without being physically present.

Measuring psychological safety

As we learned in Chapter 12, using data to quantify what is unseen but still felt can provide huge insights into our teams and organizations. It can also make talking about uncomfortable things, such as feelings and emotions, more manageable when we share a common vocabulary and can focus on numbers instead of people.

Psychological safety is best measured by anonymous survey, and it should be measured often. There are many companies that can help you do this, often as a part of larger employee engagement surveys. They usually use pulse surveys that are distributed at regular intervals (monthly or quarterly) to deliver up-to-date insights on how your teams are feeling.

Most surveys related to psychological safety are similar to the one originally designed by Amy Edmondson.[10] Participants are asked to rank a number of statements on a 5- or 7-point Likert scale, ranging from 'strongly agree' to 'strongly disagree'. The wording of three of the statements (1, 3 and 5) are written in the negative, so it is important to reverse these scores before compiling the data. Edmondson's original survey includes these statements:

1) If you make a mistake on this team, it is often held against you.
2) Members of this team are able to bring up problems and tough issues.
3) People on this team sometimes reject others for being different.
4) It is safe to take a risk on this team.
5) It is difficult to ask other members of this team for help.
6) No one on this team would deliberately act in a way that undermines my efforts.
7) Working with members of this team, my unique skills and talents are valued and utilized.

Press UNMUTE

- Consider how you can reduce social distance in your team by analyzing the SPLIT (Structure, Processes, Language, Identity and Technology) that your company employs globally.
- Commit to creating psychologically safe teams that promote conscious and candid communication.
- Help leaders develop the interpersonal skills necessary to lead psychologically safe teams.
- Measure your progress with regular pulse surveys and continue working towards safe, inclusive, connected environments. This is a long-term strategy, not a quick fix.

14

🎤 Human skills that build connection

'I hope to teach empathy skills one day, once I myself have developed a
true understanding of what that means.'[1]
Sophia, the robot from Hanson Robotics Ltd

It will be interesting to see if that day ever comes.

There are certain skills that I like to believe are uniquely human
and irreplaceable. As AI, deep learning and natural language
processing all make our lives 'smarter', technology still can't feel
or interact with humans the way we do. They will always be a close
second.

As the world becomes more automated, the only thing that sets
us apart are the skills that make us human. In this chapter, we'll
look specifically at the human skills that allow us to connect and
build stronger, more open and trusting relationships. From these
relationships, we can build a connected community that supports
unmuted communication. We will focus on the interpersonal skills
we should consider enhancing and improving in ourselves and our
teams.

Showing humility

Humility is truly a virtue in the unmuted workplace. No one can
possibly have all the answers. If bosses are viewed as always knowing
what is right, then team members will never speak up with new ideas.

The assumption is that, if it was a good idea, the boss would have already thought about it.

We are truly living in an unpredictable world. Natural disasters, political unrest and pandemics are just three of the many global challenges that have toppled markets and made us face uncertainty in recent years. None of us have a crystal ball, and our planning horizon is getting shorter and shorter. It's much better to admit to not knowing than to give an uninformed answer that could have negative consequences.

'Not knowing' needs to be reframed in the office. By admitting you don't have all the answers, you are showing that you support a learning culture where there's always room to grow. You also recognize individuals for their unique expertise and draw on the collective intelligence of the group. You hired these people for a reason. Give them the chance to shine! Here are a few suggestions of how to do this:

- 'I really can't say. Do you have any ideas?'
- 'I'm not sure. Let's brainstorm some solutions.'
- 'I have no idea. Who's the expert on this?'
- 'I don't know. Let's take some time to think about it.'

Acknowledging contribution

The unmuted workplace allows for everyone's voice to be heard. You may not always agree with what is said, but you should always acknowledge it and the courage it took for the person to express it. A simple 'thank you' is all it takes to make someone feel like they were heard, such as:

- 'Thanks so much for bringing that up.'
- 'That's a great point.'
- 'Thank you for sharing your thoughts on this.'

- 'Thanks for that. You've really given us something to think about.'
- 'Those are some great questions.'
- 'I hadn't thought about that.'
- 'Good thinking. Let's talk about that.'
- 'Wow. This was a great brainstorm. Thanks for all the fabulous ideas.'

Asking curious questions

When we approach conversations with an eagerness to learn from one another, unmuted conversations are filled with curious questions that make people think, build on what has been said and entice people to add more to the conversation. Curious questions can never be answered with 'yes' or 'no' or some other short phrase or single sentence. Their answers require us to dig deeper, think harder, challenge our thoughts and opinions and raise the group's collective intelligence. If we want to achieve more in our teams, we must start asking better questions. In the table below, there are some questions that will encourage unmuted conversations.

Table 14.1 Curious Questions

Clarify	Uncover Assumptions (our own or another's)
'Can you tell me more?'	'What assumptions might we be making here?'
'Can you explain that to me?'	
'Could you rephrase what you just said?'	'What do you see that I don't?'
Support	**Move the Idea Forward**
'What can we do to help?'	'What happens next?'
'How can we make this happen?'	'Where do we go from here?'
Have Meaning	**Expand the Conversation**
'Why is this important to you?'	'What if…?'
'Who does this serve?'	'How can we build on that?'
	'What can we learn from this?'

Encouraging participation

When participants speak for nearly equal amounts of time, the team will be consistently more effective than when certain members dominate.[2] This alone makes it clear that we need to manage conversational turns and ensure that everyone gets an equal chance to speak.

Just because someone is introverted, it doesn't mean that they don't have anything to say. If someone doesn't speak English as well as you, it doesn't mean they don't have great ideas. Just because someone comes from a culture that is stereotypically 'less direct' doesn't mean they don't have an opinion.

If you create a psychologically safe space where people feel comfortable to contribute, you will find that everyone will have something important to say. Giving everyone their turn and being patient with responses allows a safe space for everyone to participate. Here are some important actions to consider when encouraging participation:

Balancing for inclusion

Professor Tsedal Neeley has a perfect way of explaining how to manage talk time in meetings. She calls it 'balancing for inclusion'.[3]

People who tend to talk a lot (probably because of their comfort and fluency in the language) need to 'dial down their dominance'. They should listen more, check for understanding often and give others the space to speak. Basically, they need to press mute once in a while.

Those who are typically quieter, who are not as comfortable with the language or who have a fear of speaking up for whatever reason need to 'dial up engagement'. They need to add to the conversation more than they typically would.

The team leader or meeting facilitator's job is to 'balance for inclusion'. They monitor those who have not been heard and invite them into the conversation. They take responsibility for asking dominant members to dial it down or quiet members to 'dial up' if people forget to self-regulate.

Becoming an ally

There will always be situations when someone breaks the rules, oversteps and says something they shouldn't. It could be as simple as interrupting and cutting someone off, or maybe comments start to get too personal or someone isn't being self-aware and slips a microaggression into the conversation. We all need to be responsible for calling out bad behaviour and rebuilding trust in the group. Here are some phrases that might help:

Dealing with interruptions
- 'I'm not finished.'
- 'Wait. Let's let them finish.'
- 'I'm not sure they were finished...'

Dealing with attacks and microaggressions
- 'Let's keep it focused on the project, not the person.'
- 'That's not appropriate.'
- 'Can you rephrase what you just said in a more respectful way?'
- 'Please show respect for everyone here.'

Adapting to culture and context

One of the most important human skills we possess is the ability to authentically adapt to and synchronize with others. Unmuted conversations require us to 'read the room' and participate with all our senses. How do people feel? What is the overall mood? What is acceptable behaviour in this context? This is not only important in cross-cultural contexts. As we discussed in Chapter 2, intercultural challenges are also found in interpersonal relationships within the same culture. We should enter every conversation with openness and curiosity.

When you are open to feeling and understanding the detailed context and culture of the room you are in, you can better mirror, match and adapt to others. By doing so, you can connect and communicate with them effectively. As you watch others, adapt your behaviour and communication style appropriately. Here are some things to consider as you choose how to adapt:

- Formality of the hierarchy and signs of respect
- Volume and pace of the conversation
- Posture and seating style – formal or informal? Relaxed or stiff?
- Level of language and fluency
- Eye contact
- Direct or indirect communication style
- Comfort with silence
- Turn-taking rules

Listening

We talked about listening in detail in Chapter 4, but it's worth an extra reminder here. We all need to be conscious of our poor listening habits and make an effort to really pay attention with an open mind. Are you still displaying some of these bad habits?

- Judging instead of listening
- Finishing the speaker's thoughts
- Solving the speaker's problem
- Taking things personally
- Losing focus and getting distracted

So how do you become a better listener? The best listeners are those who enter conversations with no agenda other than to be curious and learn something new. They are not there to judge, but have a natural interest in people, their ideas and how they see the world. They listen more than they speak, and somehow still make the biggest impression. Many people have long held the (inaccurate) belief that the loudest, most dominant speaker is the most knowledgeable or powerful. It's time to start releasing that outdated view and let power rest with those who are there to listen, understand and carry conversations forward.

A good listener also sees the best in people. They give others the benefit of the doubt. They don't take things personally or get defensive but try to see an issue from the speaker's perspective and with their best intentions in mind. Often, we can be triggered by something a speaker says, and it has nothing to do with the speaker. The self-aware listener understands that.

Giving feedback

The days of fake 'sandwich' feedback (wrapping a negative message in praise) are over. Everyone knows the trick of starting with something nice just so you can slam them in the middle and then hope they forget when you say something sweet at the end. We see right through you, boss.

In an unmuted culture, feedback should be an easier process. If you focus on the problem and not the person, there is little need for others to become defensive or let ego get in the way. Debate should be a common practice. Every piece of feedback is a learning moment, and if this is stressed, it will be easier to use that framing when discussing difficult feedback.

The idea of feedback isn't to point out fault and make someone feel bad. It should always come from a place of care and sincere interest in helping another person. At the same time, check your ego and your culture to make sure it's your job to give feedback, that it is warranted, and not that it is just your opinion or 'gut feeling'.

Use facts and examples to support any opinions or feelings you might have and be willing to discuss and brainstorm possible alternative solutions or behaviours for the future.

Expressing disagreement

Having an unmuted culture does not mean that everyone will always agree. We won't always like everything everyone says, and we shouldn't expect to. In fact, the opposite of an unmuted culture is when everyone pretends they agree all the time and they don't feel comfortable expressing disagreement.

The key is to reframe disagreement by offering alternative viewpoints. It isn't good enough to just say, 'I don't like that idea.' You need to be able to offer an alternative idea or solution. If you really don't think something is a good idea, invite people to view the issue from a different perspective.

Standing up for what's right

Our digital world connects us more than ever before and gives everyone a voice. Movements such as #MeToo and #BlackLivesMatter swept across the world, showing the impact our voices can have when we have the courage to speak up.

An unmuted culture requires us to speak up, especially when we see injustice. The 2021 Edelman Trust report found that the public expect CEOs to take a stand on social issues now that trust in government has been lost.

Each one of us needs to be ready to take a stand. In order to do that, you need to know what you stand for. What are your values and your mission in the world? What makes you uniquely you? What injustice is worth fighting for?

Apply your human skills to stand up for what's right at home, in your community, at work and on the world stage. That's what it truly means to be unmuted.

Press UNMUTE

- Human skills are more important than ever as the world becomes more automated. Those who improve their interpersonal skills will have the greatest advantage in the future of work.
- The foundation of human skills is caring about others. When you make this your priority, and enter conversations with the best intentions in mind, your natural skills for empathy and understanding will shine through.
- Keep an open mind, listen fully and make an effort to understand the best intentions of others.

🎤 Connecting online – the new netiquette

'You've got mail!'

It was the early 1990s and my parents had just bought our first dial-up modem. I can remember the anticipation as we waited what seemed like an eternity through all the beeps, scratches and static as it attempted to connect us to this new thing called the Internet. When our America Online connection was finally secure, those three simple words, 'You've got mail!' were all the reward one needed for the long wait.

Fast forward 30 years and I don't think anyone is excited to turn on their computer to an inbox full of email. We are in a state of information overload and constant connection. The pandemic has only made this worse. From February 2020 to February 2021 there was an increase of 40.6 billion emails sent through Microsoft Exchange Online.[1] And that is just one of many email providers.

Over the past 30 years (and for some early adopters, 40 years or more) the ways we communicate online have radically changed. From network servers to mail lists to email and social media, now we can stay connected to everyone everywhere with just the click of a mouse – or trackpad.

When COVID-19 lockdowns began, the Internet is what saved us and allowed us to keep our economies running. Work from home became the norm and everyone struggled to do their best to adapt to a new normal. This included a significant increase in the number of video calls we were expected to participate in from home. While balancing the comforts of home with our professional working life, many of us forgot some common courtesies. Most people realized they should show up to virtual meetings the same way they showed up to work. Maybe they wouldn't be quite as formal, but at least good enough for casual Friday. Still, there were people showing up in their pyjamas or saying they couldn't turn on their cameras because they weren't dressed appropriately.

Most companies didn't have communication guidelines in place that covered these situations. If they did, it seems no one had read them. We needed new rules of online etiquette.

The way we interact with each other online has been cause for concern since the first computer networks were used in the 1980s. Seeing a need for a general code of conduct, Chuq Von Rospach worked with a group of about 15 concerned Usenet members to publish *A Primer on How to Work with the USENET Community*.[2]

As Chuq explained to me, it was an 'early act of crowdsourcing (long before anyone invented that word), creating a public domain document that was basically freeware (before anyone invented that word), to help people manage online communities and social networks (long before anyone invented those words)'.[3]

They had compiled the first code of conduct for online communication, and Chuq came up with a name for it too: 'netiquette' – a hybrid of 'network' and 'etiquette'. In the 2020s the term 'netiquette' has suddenly expanded to include video conferencing, instant messaging and online social networking.

Regardless of the technology, all online etiquette can be summarized in the first recommendation of Chuq's 1984 primer: 'Never forget that the person on the other side is human.'[4]

In 1995, Virginia Shea published a book based on Chuq's primer called *Netiquette* in which she added a follow-up guideline to this first point: 'Adhere to the same standards of behaviour online that you follow in real life.'[5]

Shirley Taylor, a business-writing specialist, brought netiquette into the new millennium in her 2009 book *E-Mail Etiquette,* where she dedicated a chapter to 'Nurturing E-Mail Netiquette' and fighting the 'Seven Deadly Sins of E-Mail Netiquette'. She reminds writers to focus on the relationship by avoiding jargon, showing empathy and focusing on the human touch, along with many other tips and strategies to improve online business communication.[6]

Unprecedented change

As the whole world transitioned to working online in the course of about two months, we saw digital communication change faster than ever before. As Microsoft CEO Satya Nadella famously shared in early 2020, 'We've seen two years' worth of digital transformation in two months.'[7]

We had to make some decisions about how to lead teams that were suddenly dispersed, off balance and needing direction. It didn't take long before a new netiquette began developing around our online, on-camera communications. I began working with regional leadership teams to design best practices that would help them raise the level of their own communication and set standards and expectations for their teams.

To be honest, we were making it up as we went along. We leaned on research on human behaviour, psychology and emotional intelligence, and combined it with a dose of common sense. We had conversations with leaders so that they could unmute from the top down and be role models for their teams. We surveyed employees and listened to their needs.

Designing a virtual toolkit

The outcome was a virtual toolkit to supplement internal company communication policies. The toolkit is just that – a group of tools. It was never presented as 'rules' or 'guidelines' or 'musts'. The toolkit gives friendly recommendations, outlines best practices and leaves the rest up to the individual to implement. In global companies, it's important that this guide is generic enough that it can be customized to specific regions and cultural differences (e.g. dress code, scheduling, break times, etc.). If your company doesn't have a virtual toolkit, consider compiling one with the following components:

Best practices guide

The best practices guide aligns with the corporate values and shows the benefits of having a strong professional presence in virtual meetings or presentations, both internally and externally. This guide answers questions around your company's recommendations for:

- Dress code
- Backgrounds (and includes approved corporate backgrounds)
- Basic camera and microphone set-up
- Verbal, vocal and visual pointers to communicate with confidence
- Engagement tools that are approved by your IT department (external polls, whiteboards, brainstorming software)
- Break times and scheduling within and across time zones

Pre-event checklist

When you are quickly moving from call to call, it helps to have a short checklist of even the most obvious reminders so that you can quickly prepare yourself for the next meeting. Print the checklist on a small card and place it on your desk. Here are some of the things included on my checklist:

- Pause all file-syncing programs to save bandwidth
- Turn phone to silent (and no vibration)
- Turn off all other alerts and notifications
- Get water/coffee/tea

- Clear the computer desktop of all open files in case I need to share my screen
- Prepare and open files I know I'll need to share
- Check lighting, camera and microphone settings
- Turn off wifi and plug into my broadband connection
- Alert those around me that I'll be on a call and to please not disturb

Platform quick-start guide

If you've recently changed systems or have new employees, a quick-start guide can help your team (or external stakeholders joining your calls) connect to your virtual meeting platform with ease. It should include basics such as:

- How to join a call, and the passwords or codes needed (if any)
- Any downloads that are necessary
- Where to find camera and microphone settings
- How to use the chat box and share screen functions
- How to set a virtual background

Online event invitation template

Standardize your company invitations and make a great first impression by creating a template for online events. This ensures that all the important information is sent the first time. Your template should include:

- Proper salutation: 'Dear _____'
- Agenda
- Any files that need to be reviewed prior to the meeting
- Expectations: Will the call be on camera? Should people login early?
- Platform link and log-in instructions
- Contact person (with phone number), in case of difficulties joining the meeting

Tools and tasks table

Communication channels are getting smarter (literally) with the introduction of artificially intelligent tools, but they aren't always making us more productive. With information coming at us from every direction, it can often take more time and energy to find the information we are searching for. Teams need to decide the tools they are going to use and be selective about the information they send and where they send it. A tools and tasks table can help to streamline your communication.

Make a list of the tasks you typically perform. Then decide the tool that is the best fit for that task. Global teams should also consider the agreed timing for certain types of communication based on location and time zones.

Below is an example of a simple table a client developed for their regional APAC team.

Table 15.1 Sample Tools and Tasks Table

TASK	TOOL	TIMING
Team meetings Client calls	MS Teams	Be respectful of time zones and normal working hours Avoid Friday evenings
Larger meetings with 20+ participants	Webex	Appropriate timing to fit all time zones
Larger meetings with 100+ participants	Webex Events	Appropriate timing to fit all time zones
File collaboration	SharePoint	Updates/edits can be made at any time
Project chat groups	MS Teams	Office hours
Social groups Informal Check-ins	MS Teams	Agree to appropriate timing in group
Formal messages Confidential documents	Email	Office hours of recipient. Use 'delay send' if necessary
Important, time-sensitive conversations Informal check-ins	Telephone	Flexible depending on situation, but try to stay in office hours

Other considerations

Here are some other categories you may wish to include in your virtual toolkit:

Manager's guide

Some companies include a manager's guide with more detailed information for managing dispersed staff. Managers need to lead by example and understand that there are higher expectations of them.

Security overview

If you have a strict global IT department and there are certain restrictions on your system, a security overview is a nice addition to your toolkit. List the company-approved software applications and clarify the risk of using non-approved solutions.

Additional training

Depending on the current comfort levels of your team, you might consider supplementing the toolkit with training to raise your team's confidence on camera, help them present and engage audiences online and allow them to conduct more effective virtual meetings.

New netiquette guide

I've attempted to update the 1984 and 1995 network etiquette guides for the twenty-first century. Below is an overview, with each point in more detail in the next section. You will need to customize this guide to incorporate your company's values and make it meaningful to your team members.

1) Be conscious of the human behind the screen.
2) Show up and behave online the same way you would in person.
3) Choose the right communication channel.
4) Respect people's time.
5) Give more than you gain; listen more than you speak.
6) Put your audience first.
7) Respect people's privacy.
8) Give credit where it is due.
9) Check your sources.
10) Build relationships; don't spam.

The New Netiquette

A lot has changed online since 1984 and Chuq Von Rospach's first attempt at writing a basic netiquette for the Usenet community. One thing that has not changed is that we are all still human. The points that Virginia Shea reiterated in 1995 and Shirley Taylor continued to build on in 2009 are all still relevant. Here is my suggestion for a new netiquette updated for the 2020s and beyond.

If you want to build strong relationships in the digital age that support an unmuted culture, you need to be a good human that cares about others and the way you make them feel. This should be true whether you are building a relationship face to face or over the Internet. By building a community that agrees to a certain code of conduct, you can create more trust and connection in the community itself.

1. Be conscious of the human behind the screen
Breathe before you reply to that email or social media post. Don't write anything that you wouldn't say to the person's face, or mind having on the front page of your favourite newspaper. The Internet is forever.

2. Show up and behave online the same way you would in person
Be ethical. Don't do anything illegal. Change out of your pyjamas. Take pride in your appearance. Treat people with respect. Say 'hello' when you enter a (virtual) room. Wait your turn to speak. Listen. Build relationships.

3. Choose the right communication channel
Think about whether something should be mentioned publicly in a chat group or privately in an email. What are you trying to achieve, and what's the best way to communicate it? Is this something that can be addressed in an email, or should you pick up the phone?

4. Respect people's time

Keep online interactions and meetings short. Have a clear agenda and don't waste anyone's time. Be prepared. Show up on time. Have files open and ready to share. Check your tech before you join a call.

5. Give more than you gain; listen more than you speak

The Internet gives us a public platform unlike any other. Share your unique voice with the world. Be generous in sharing and helping others, but also take time to listen.

6. Put your audience first

Keep time zones in mind when scheduling meetings. Check shared calendars to avoid double-booking someone. Let people turn off their cameras if they aren't expected to participate. Be a conscious communicator who puts your audience at ease and is respectful of cultural and interpersonal differences. Be careful with humour and sarcasm.

7. Respect people's privacy

You don't need to be a newscaster. Don't announce the birth of your cousin's new baby before she does, or your friend's engagement, or the death of a family member before you are sure everyone has been informed in real life. Ask for permission to post pictures from a dinner with friends, especially if children are in them. Not everyone wants a public digital fingerprint.

8. Give credit where it is due

Don't steal people's content. Don't take credit for other people's work. Make sources clear.

9. Check your sources

Don't spread fake news. Check where your information comes from. Even information you are sure is true, because you've seen it posted 1,000 times, is not necessarily true.

10. Build relationships; don't spam

Don't connect with people just to sell to them. Don't add email addresses to your mailing list without permission. Follow the rules in groups and only post relevant information in group chats.

Press UNMUTE

- Develop a virtual toolkit as a supplement to your company's communication policies.
- Write a netiquette code that incorporates your company values and which everyone is committed to following.
- Be a good human, both online and offline.

🎙 PART IV: UNMUTE

16

🎤 Unmuting yourself

'We can't hear you...
Nope...
Still can't...
Maybe check your audio settings...??'

I wish it were that easy – just find the audio settings and press unmute! Unfortunately, real life is a bit more complicated than virtual meetings, and we have a few more steps to take before we can transform ourselves, our families, our teams and our communities.

Solving communication and collaboration problems is not as simple as holding a team-building day or providing some communication skills training. The challenges run deeper and their inter-relations directly affect other parts of the puzzle.

Pressing unmute is a long-term commitment that will either need improvements, maintenance or both.

No matter your place in an organization, we can all work together to unmute in our own lives and teams. Here are specific actions that you can begin to take today to become a more conscious, confident and connected communicator.

Becoming a conscious communicator

TOO LOUD? Work on self-awareness and cultural intelligence

The person who lacks self-awareness and is not a conscious communicator will end up being *too loud* for their environment. They dominate conversations and are often unknowingly offensive. Their

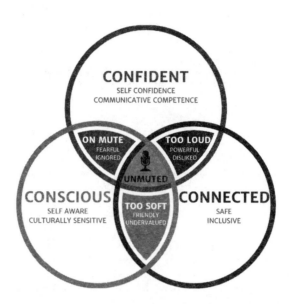

fast-thinking brains are making all the decisions, even though they (more than anyone else) think they only speak the truth and make logical, rational decisions.

The combination of confidence with a connected and supportive environment allows for the non-conscious communicator to take control. What's worse, many of these people will be supported and be seen as leaders, especially in the Western world, where confidence and eloquence are typically seen as powerful leadership traits.

A conscious communicator, on the other hand, recognizes, respects and embraces difference. They accept, acknowledge and celebrate all members of a team, leading to more inclusion in the workplace.

When you are a conscious communicator, you can be true to yourself, your values and ideas, while also respecting others.

Here are some ways you can work on becoming a more conscious communicator:

Assessments and profiles

To begin getting a better idea of what makes you think, feel and behave the way you do, investigate some personality profiles or other mindset profiles, such as the Global DISC. These will help you discover your typical preferences and behaviours.[1] Encourage others on your team to do the same and then map out the team scores to see where you overlap and where you are different. Discuss how this affects your team's communication and working styles.

Armed with this knowledge, you can begin to enter conversations and other interactions with more self-awareness. This is where you can begin to increase your metacognitive evaluation of your surroundings (Chapter 3). You'll be able to watch the other people around you and see how they act and react and whether this aligns with you and your preferences.

Why do you react differently than they do? What is it about the way you see the world that makes you think, feel and behave differently? Most importantly, what do they see in the world that you don't? They also have a unique view and unless you truly understand it, you will not fully connect and empathize with them.

Write your new story

Along with profiles and metacognitive processes, you consider the identity narrative you have been telling yourself. Think about the stories of your life that you have chosen to define you. Do they serve you well? Could different stories help you to step into a new role or challenge?

You cannot begin to think differently without acting differently (Chapter 1), and stories of your past will not have the lessons that you need to step out of your comfort zone. Challenge yourself to try new things, meet new people and adjust your behaviours. Celebrate any failures as signs that you are trying new things.

Approach others with care and curiosity

Begin approaching all your interpersonal relationships with the same care and curiosity you would show in an intercultural relationship. Don't assume that simply because you're from the same place, you must have similar values and beliefs. If that were the case, we would all agree on the best candidate during political elections!

Be especially aware of microinequities and be prepared to speak up if someone says or does something that could be viewed as offensive. Be courageous to call people out, but also be forgiving once awareness has been raised.

Sit down with your team to discuss microinequities. Make a list of comments or actions that people have taken offence to. Discuss why these could make some people feel as though they aren't accepted in the group. Write rules of engagement around how you speak and interact in meetings, over the internet or any other communication channels you might use.

Don't be afraid to authentically adapt and meet people halfway

Every culture has some variation of the 'Golden Rule': treat others the way that you would like to be treated. If you stop to think about it, it's a little self-centred to assume that everyone wants to be treated the way you want to be treated. Authenticity is important but being able to adapt and meet others halfway is even more so. The more self-aware you are, the easier it will be to read and understand others.

Ask for feedback and be willing to accept it

You won't know what others truly think of you until you ask. Asking for and listening to honest feedback can be difficult. Knowing how others view you instead of how you *think* they view you can be the greatest gift for self-improvement.

Listen

Actively work on becoming a more conscious listener. Ask curious questions, enter conversations with a learning mindset and listen to what isn't being said.

Record meetings and presentations (with permission)

You'll hate every second of this because the way we sound and present ourselves always feels different from an audience perspective. Are you dominating the meeting or do you barely speak up? What kind of language do you use? Did you say anything that could have been offensive? Take advantage of technology and apply artificial intelligence to get a non-biased assessment of your speaking style. Online tools like Yoodli can help to quantify your progress.[2]

Becoming a confident communicator

TOO SOFT? Build confidence in your *self* and your *skills*
We know that equal contribution by team members is directly related to more effective and high-performing teams. This is why you can't afford to turn down the volume on your ideas.

Here are some actions you can take to increase your confidence:

Confidence in your self

- Identify what triggers anxiety or stops you from expressing yourself.
- Prepare for situations where you know you'll be asked to speak: organize your thoughts, make notes and practise answering questions you think you could be asked.
- Pep talks work. Try putting yourself into a positive emotional state before entering a meeting or presentation.
- Take care of yourself. Feeling good in your body helps you feel better about yourself.
- Share your successes and celebrate other's success too.
- Develop a strong group of friends and colleagues who support and encourage you.
- Get a coach or mentor (or both) for support and to help you see how amazing you are.
- Pay it forward. Encourage others around you to speak up and be seen. Recognize their talents and give them opportunities to shine.

Confidence in your skills
Connection not perfection
If you are reading this book in English, then I can guarantee your English is good enough for global business. Of course it is important

to have a strong foundation in English, but more important is how well you connect with people through English. Use simple words and phrases. Add your personality and energy to your message through body language, facial expressions and your tone of voice. You are the only one holding you back from communicating with confidence.

If English is your only language or you were lucky enough to grow up with English, meet your colleagues halfway. Listen to the person behind the language. Connect with their message. Make an effort to understand.

Body language and voice

Set up your virtual 'studio' so that you make a great impression online. Think about your framing, lighting, microphone and camera before you get on a call. Practise with a friend or colleague to make sure you know how to use the technology. If you aren't fully confident with a piece of technology, *don't use it*! It is better to keep things simple and professional than try to wow your audience, only for it to end in technology failures.

In person, communication is a full-body sport. Use gestures. Make appropriate eye contact. Remember to be self-aware. In some cultures, too much movement could be seen as less competent or overly emotional. Try to match the style of the room you are with.

Use your voice as a tool. Emphasize words by adding emotion to your voice. Make your voice interesting to listen to, especially on virtual calls. Doing so will hold the attention of your listeners longer.

Embrace 'bad' English

Speak simply. Learn how to explain what you do and know clearly and concisely. Avoid idioms, jargon and highly technical terms. Monitor your pace. Speak slowly enough that everyone can follow. Do not judge people based on how they use English or what their English sounds like. Have patience.

Get comfortable with different varieties of English
Take a course in accent recognition to better prepare yourself for working with people from all over the world. If a course isn't available, increase your accented English input. For example, watch TEDx Talks by people from different countries (if they are in English) or find famous people from that language background who have done television interviews. If you can find a talk radio station in English in that country, listen to it. Watch movies and listen to music in foreign languages so you are familiar with the sounds of other languages as well. Foreign words will sometimes make an appearance in a person's English. There is a lot you can do to get comfortable with the many varieties of English spoken all over the world.

Becoming a connected communicator

ON MUTE? Work on changing your environment or rising above it
If you are conscious and confident, you will have the challenge of presenting your message in a world that is not always connected or compassionate. When we fear repercussions for speaking up, even the most confident people can end up pressing mute. Maybe you've tried to speak up, but no one is listening. Worse, perhaps you've been ostracized from the group because you stood up for yourself or didn't agree to adapt to a culture you don't believe in.

On the world stage, we can't use a poor environment as an excuse. The Internet and social media have offered everyone a public stage, and we know the world can be cruel and divisive. Still, it is expected that leaders in the private sector have a public voice.

Celebrity status has been bestowed upon CEOs since the times of Henry Ford and John D. Rockefeller. Today, our digital connectedness, the amplification of voices by the media and the speed at which information travels, gives powerful business leaders (and upcoming leaders) an easy way to get attention and gain a following. The same is true for thought leaders and university researchers.

This change in the way information travels the world can be a blessing or a curse. It enables the voices of the typically oppressed and silenced, but it also carries the risk of extreme judgement and 'cancel culture'. As quickly as a new influencer rises to the top, they can also be shot right back down.

There is always inherent risk when pressing unmute. Use your self-awareness and cultural intelligence to present yourself and your ideas in a way that is as appealing as possible to dissenting views. But that dissention will still be there. You must courageously believe that the importance of your message outweighs this risk.

In the workplace, it's up to your leadership to lay the foundation for an unmuted communication culture. It is easy to feel helpless when you are in a toxic environment. How can you create a safe space for unmuted expression if the leadership cuts down your ideas, won't listen or doesn't take your concerns seriously?

Even if your leaders aren't on board, there are many things you can do to enhance your relationships and create more connection in your environments:

Focus on your relationships

How much time do you dedicate to strengthening your relationships? Are you so focused on your results that you don't prioritize the people that help you achieve them? Building relationships is as much a part of your job as the work itself. You'll find that when you have better relationships, the work will be easier, you'll have more support and you'll always have the right person to turn to for help.

Put time in your calendar to connect with people. It could be as simple as a quick call or message to see how someone is doing. Remember the 'difficult' people too. These are the ones you should spend even more time with so that you can try to understand them better. 'Difficult' only means 'different'. If you can understand what drives them and how they see the world, you'll find it easier to work with them.

Ask everyone to contribute

You don't have to be the person leading a meeting or team to ask people to contribute. Watch for people who are hiding in the shadows or are being overlooked. Ask for their opinion. A simple 'What do you think, Sally?' is all it takes to give someone permission to open up and share what they are thinking.

Have a curious learning mentality

Enter every conversation with a curious mindset. You may think you have all the answers, and maybe you do, but take a moment to see the world from someone else's perspective. There could be something you missed. There is always something new to discover – about yourself, the other person or the world around you.

Reframe failure for yourself and others

Start talking about failure. Remember Sara Blakely's dad asking her how she failed that week (see Chapter 13)? Set a goal to fail at something every week. This will mean you tried many new things (you won't fail at all of them), and it's only through trying that you can grow.

Let your new love of failure rub off on those around you. Ask people about their failures as much as you ask about their successes. You will probably learn a lot more!

Discuss rules of engagement

To improve the quality of your meetings, ask your team to discuss some basic rules of engagement. This could be done formally with company guidelines, or it could just be a quick, informal discussion at the beginning of a meeting. If you've had an open discussion about the rules, it's much easier to stop someone when they infringe upon them. Some of the rules you might agree to could be:

- No interruptions
- Be clear and concise (perhaps even give time limits)

- Stick to the agenda
- Everyone speaks
- Call out microinequities if you hear any
- End five minutes early

Just say it

Change needs to start somewhere, and if you are in a toxic environment, how much worse can it get? Speak up to a manager or your human resources department to voice your concerns. Sometimes, the boss just isn't aware that their behaviour has been creating a poor environment.

As you work on the three areas of the Unmuted Framework, know that this is a work in progress. There are always ways we can improve. You will never reach a state of total self-awareness. You will always feel fear. We can only show up as our best selves and do the best we can.

17

🎙 Unmuting your organization

It is very difficult to have an unmuted culture at work if the leadership is not fully on board and leading by example. It takes commitment from the leaders to encourage people to speak up and to create safe, open environments where people aren't fearful. If you say you want people to unmute, but then respond negatively every time they do, you won't get very far.

Focus on building stronger, more empathetic relationships with your team. Show people that it's okay to be vulnerable and admit when you make mistakes. The success of an unmuted workplace is dependent on how much the team trusts *you* as a leader.

If someone comes to you with a complaint, take it seriously and act immediately. If someone makes a mistake, treat it as a learning experience and find a positive way to move forward. If someone shares a great new idea or discloses something personal, acknowledge them and really listen.

The roles of an unmuted leader

The unmuted leader needs to transform their leadership style to encourage and enhance an unmuted workplace. There are new roles you'll need to embrace so that everyone can show up, speak up and contribute fully to the organization.

Adviser

Develop the systems and standards that will support an unmuted culture. Your adviser role defines how you manage and interact with your team. As an adviser you should:

- Explain to your team why speaking up is important.
- Connect an unmuted culture to your company goals and vision.

- In collaboration with your team, develop guidelines or 'rules of engagement' for your meetings that ensure acceptance, inclusion and efficiency.
- Manage discussions and step in if complaints or criticisms are getting personal instead of focusing on a project.
- Introduce new vocabulary and a new mindset concerning failure.
- Create structures and processes for speaking up.
- Call out microinequities and help the team learn from them.

Cheerleader

You are the best person to encourage your people to speak up. Consider how you react and respond when people contribute (or complain). Your actions and reactions will determine how much people participate.

- Ask great questions from a place of curiosity, not judgement.
- Encourage team members to challenge your (and each other's) ideas and go deeper with idea generation.
- Celebrate intelligent failures.
- Acknowledge people and their ideas. Express gratitude to your team.
- Balance meeting discussions so everyone has a chance to speak. Make space for quieter team members to share their ideas.
- Stop interrupting.
- Trust your unmuted team. If you show trust, they will be more willing to trust you.

Peer

You need to walk the talk in your interactions with your team. Lead by example. Show humility, vulnerability and empathy. Be a human first and a boss second. Here's how.

- Model vulnerability and authenticity. Disclose more about yourself to your team and get to know them as people.

- Offer input and show that you're listening. Close your computer during meetings!
- Admit your mistakes and share your stories of failure so the team can see it's important to learn from our mistakes.
- Build stronger relationships with team members – build your brain and heart trust.

Student

You should be constantly learning about your people, their needs and the overall mood of the team. Ongoing measurement and self-reflection are needed to maintain an unmuted culture. Always be learning.

- Conduct cultural assessments of team members and get to know each other's working styles, personalities and cultural attributes.
- Map your interpersonal communication networks to identify and engage with influencers and find vulnerabilities.
- Measure the psychological safety of your team regularly through pulse surveys.
- Ask for clarification when you need it and make it clear that it's always okay to ask questions.
- Approach conversations with a learning mindset and curiosity.

Unmuted initiatives to connect with your team

What specific changes can you make to raise awareness, create more psychological safety and encourage members of your team to unmute? Here are some initiatives you could set in motion to begin pressing UNMUTE in your company.

Informal check-ins

Schedule time in your calendar for informal check-ins with your direct reports. These meetings are not meant to focus specifically on work, but life in general. Of course, conversation will likely turn to work concerns, and that's fine too. The point is to have an informal outlet where you can learn about your people and connect.

This could take the form of a 'walk and talk' where you do something active and beneficial for both of you (and get those daily steps in) while catching up. If you are working remotely, it might be a virtual coffee meeting or a Friday happy hour at the end of the week. One-on-ones are best, but depending on the number of your direct reports, small group activities can also work.

Office hours

Set aside a few hours each week that are always open for others to call on you. Even if you have an 'open door policy', people might be worried they'll disturb you. If you set aside empty time that is only for the purpose of helping, answering questions and fielding concerns, you might get a better response. Keep in mind that some people still won't approach you, so take the time to reach out to them too.

Weekly messages

If you have a larger team or want to reach more levels of the company, consider sending out a weekly message. Emails are often ignored or deleted, so consider doing a short video and posting it on the internal network. Be simple and authentic; don't worry about the production value. A video from your mobile phone is great. Share something more personal about your experiences over the weekend, an idea you've been thinking about, a recent failure and what you learned or a funny incident. Make these videos a highlight that your team looks forward to watching.

Reframing failure

Worst practices events

An organization called the Failure Institute organizes monthly TED-style events called Fuckup Nights in over 300 cities across 90 countries where they 'live life without filters by sharing stories of failure'.[1] They invite three or four speakers to share their biggest mistakes and failures – anything from a product recall to a partnership that fell to pieces. The bigger the mistake, the better.

How about organizing a worst practices webinar series of your own? People from all over the organization, from every part of the hierarchy, come together to share their stories of failure. That marketing campaign that bombed, the product idea that never happened, the media statement that had to be retracted and apologized for. Share the failures and what they meant to the people and the organization. Discuss the lessons learned, and celebrate the fact that at least someone tried.

How did you fail this week?

Make reframing failure a daily habit by starting your team meetings with stories of failures. Instead of what was your 'win' this week, you could ask what your biggest failure was; this will lead to a more open discussion and more vulnerability within a safe space. Try to encourage people to express what is really going on, how they are feeling, what is happening with their work and family and anything else they are comfortable sharing in those scheduled spontaneous interactions in your team meetings.

The Oops! Awards

Create a yearly award for the biggest intelligent failure. Celebrate someone (or a team) who put excellent effort into a project that just didn't work. Show that you applaud people who take calculated risks and go all in, even if they weren't a success. The more people try, the more the company will succeed. Celebrate those who try; make failure fun.

Communicating more effectively

Sometimes all it takes to communicate better is to formalize the goals and expectations we have for communication. Co-create guidelines and best practices with your teams. Talk about how people want to communicate, what is important to them when it comes to communication and how the company can support their communication efforts.

Here is a selection of communication tools, frameworks and guidelines many of my clients have implemented:

Tools and tasks tables

This simple document outlines the communication channels in your company so that people don't waste time and energy searching for the information they need. It also shows respect for people's time zones and gives guidelines around when it is appropriate to communicate. You can refer to the sample on page 146 in Chapter 15.

Rules of engagement

How we speak, write and interact with each other in meetings, email and informal gatherings are our rules of engagement. They can be a formal policy outlining communication expectations or an informal conversation at the start of a meeting to set the ground rules for discussion.

Virtual toolkit

A virtual toolkit sets expectations and provides guidance on how to show up online. As digital communication grows and teams are more distant, online interactions become much more important. Revisit Chapter 15 to take a closer look at this important tool.

Netiquette guidelines

Basic manners and respect online are also important. Our netiquette has changed over time and will continue to change with technology. Use the suggestions in Chapter 15 to design the netiquette that is appropriate for your company.

Writing guidelines and style guides

Your communication team probably follows writing guidelines and a branding style guide, but I'm always amazed how many people in the rest of the organization are unaware of it. Good writing is important for everyone in the company. Circulate best practices for email writing, client correspondence, proposals and reports. Style guides that include corporate templates also ensure consistency and professionalism across the company.

Inclusion policies

Make sure that your diversity and inclusion policies address the more invisible non-inclusive practices that can appear via communication. It is not only important to have policies concerning race, gender, age, sexuality and other minority groups, but also to point out that discrimination due to language group or accent (which are often closely tied to racial and ethnic groups) will not be tolerated. Microinequities should be specifically addressed, as well as guidelines for learning from these comments and behaviours.

Measuring growth

Unmuting is a process that is always under construction. There are many measurements available to help you better understand yourself, your team and your progress towards creating an unmuted culture. Here are some examples:

- Start with the Unmuted Assessment to get an idea of the areas where you need to focus most.
- Organizational network analysis to map the connections and communication channels within your team, department or larger organization.
- Global DISC or any number of other assessments and profiling tools to raise self-awareness and better understand team members.
- Psychological safety measurements in the form of ongoing pulse surveys for team members. These should be short, easy to answer and frequent.
- Identify training gaps and help to build capabilities and confidence to unmute.

Making improvements

As you measure and grow, you will always need to make small adjustments. You'll likely find performance gaps that can be filled by training. Helping your teams grow and develop their interpersonal/ intercultural, communication and overall human skills will lead to greater confidence and performance.

It will take an investment in the process and your people to continue along the unmuted path, and it's normal to expect bumps along the way. Regular touchpoints that keep communication a priority will help to build momentum and motivation. Consider ongoing programmes such as internal and external webinar series on topics related to conscious, confident and connected communication. Especially for remote teams, these events bring everyone together and give them a chance to interact and focus on a shared goal.

More than anything, build your awareness as a leader, and keep communication as one of your top business goals. UNMUTE yourself, and your team will follow.

🎙 Unmuted Resources

As you read this book, take advantage of the extra resources that have been developed to help you unmute yourself and your organization:

Unmuted Assessment

Are you too loud, too quiet, or on mute? This assessment will show you where you fall along the three axes of the Unmuted Framework and provide you with ideas for getting started. Take this assessment before reading the book to find out what might be holding you back from truly unmuting yourself and your team.

Unmuted Discussion Guides

As you read *Unmuted*, pause to access the Unmuted Discussion Guides found at the end of each chapter. Each guide consists of a video where I walk you through the most important lessons and challenge you to dive deeper and reflect on what you have learned. Take notes on the journal handouts (pdf files) provided with each video. These guides are powerful tools for self-reflection and are especially useful if you are reading *Unmuted* with your team, with friends, or in your book club.

Unmuted Action Guide

Are you ready to transform your team, business unit, or entire organization into an UNMUTED workplace? This guide explains how to get started.

Visit www.heatherhansen.com/unmuted or scan this QR code to access all the Unmuted Resources.

🎙 Endnotes

Introduction

1. VUCA is an acronym for volatile, uncertain, complex and ambiguous and is used to describe situations that need strong leadership. Originally coined in the late 1980s, it was adopted by the United States military and then later in business to form a framework for analyzing strategy.

Chapter 1: Who are you?

1. Barb West was my Professor of Anthropology at University of the Pacific's School of International Studies from 1998–2002. I was also lucky to have her as my student adviser. She was instrumental in helping to design (and guide me through) a self-designed major in Language and Society. Today she lives in Australia and runs Culture Works, a cross-cultural communication consultancy. She's also a cultural outlier.
2. The Google search for 'Who am I?' was performed on 25 July 2021 in Singapore.
3. A reference to Steve Jobs' Stanford commencement speech, 12 June 2005. You can view this speech and read the transcript here: https://news.stanford.edu/2005/06/14/jobs-061505/
4. McAdams, D. P. 'The Psychology of Life Stories', *Review of General Psychology*, 5(2), pp. 100–12. Washington DC: American Psychological Association, 2001.
5. McAdams, D. P. and Kate McLean. 'Narrative Identity', *Current Directions in Psychological Science*, 22(3), pp. 233–8. Washington DC: American Psychological Association, 2013.
6. Hammack, Phillip L. 'Narrative and the Cultural Psychology of Identity', *Personality and Social Psychology Review*, 12(3), pp. 222–47. Washington DC: American Psychological Association, 2008.
7. Ibarra, Herminia. *Act Like a Leader, Think Like a Leader*. Boston: Harvard Business Review Press, 2015.
8. Brown, Brené. *Dare to Lead*. London: Vermilion, 2018.
9. Brown, Brené. *Daring Greatly*. London: Penguin Life, 2015.

Chapter 2: The power of perception

1. You can access this video online to see Leona Chin's driving skills and how her customers reacted to their special test drive: https://www.youtube.com/watch?v=zCQ-etiFyho
2. Zimmerman, M. (1989) 'The nervous system in the context of information theory', in: R. F. Schmidt & G. Thews (Eds) *Human Physiology* (Berlin, Springer), 166–73.
3. Kahneman, Daniel. *Thinking, Fast and Slow*. London: Penguin, 2012.
4. Todorov, Alexander, et al. 'Inferences of Competence from Faces Predict Election Outcomes', *Science*, 308 (5728), pp. 1623–26. Washington DC: American Association for the Advancement of Science, 2005.
5. Cogsdill, EJ, Todorov, AT, Spelke, ES, Banaji, MR. 'Inferring Character From Faces: A Developmental Study'. *Psychological Science*. 2014;25(5):1132–1139.

6. Taras, Vas, Piers Steel, and Bradley L. Kirkman. 'Does Country Equate with Culture? Beyond Geography in the Search for Cultural Boundaries.' *MIR: Management International Review*, 56, no. 4, pp. 455–87. 2016.
7. Toth, Csaba. *Uncommon Sense in Unusual Times*. Authors Unite Publishing, 2012.
8. Ibid.
9. Learn more about the Global DISC assessment at www.icq.global.

Chapter 3: Authentic adaptability

1. The Project Gutenberg eBook of *Alice's Adventures in Wonderland*, by Lewis Carroll. Release Date: January, 1991 [eBook #11] [Most recently updated: 12 October 2020] Language: English, Character set encoding: UTF-8, Produced by: Arthur DiBianca and David Widger
2. 2021 Edelman Trust Barometer: www.edelman.com.
3. George, Bill. *Discover Your True North*. San Francisco: Jossey-Bass Publishing, 2015.

Chapter 4: Conscious listening

1. Julian Treasure, 'How to Speak so People Want to Listen', TED Global 2013: www.ted.com/talks/julian_treasure_how_to_speak_so_that_people_want_to_listen
2. Anita Williams Woolley, et al. 'Evidence for a Collective Intelligence Factor in the Performance of Human Groups', *Science* 330, pp 686–8, 2010. View online: http://www.cs.cmu.edu/~ab/Salon/research/Woolley_et_al_Science_2010-2.pdf

Chapter 5: Unmuted inclusion

1. True story from a female, African-American friend and colleague.
2. Wing Sue, Derald, Capodilupo, Christina M., Torino, Gina C., Bucceri, Jennifer M., Holder, Aisha M. B., Nadal, Kevin L., and Esquilin, Marta. 'Racial Microaggressions in Everyday Life: Implications for Clinical Practice', *American Psychologist* 271, Vol. 62, No. 4, 271–86, May–June 2007.
3. Silvia de Anca and Salvador Aragón, 'The Three Types of Diversity that Shape Our Identities', *Harvard Business Review*, 24 May 2018.
4. Alison Reynolds, David Lewis, 'Teams solve problems faster when they are more cognitively diverse', Report in *Harvard Business Review*, 30 March 2017.
5. Jeremiah Green and John R.M. Hand, 'Diversity matters/delivers/wins revisited in S&P 500˚ firms', 19 May 2021, Available at SSRN: https://ssrn.com/abstract=3849562.
6. Leadership IQ, 'Why New Hires Fail: The Landmark "Hiring for Attitude" Study Updated with New Data', June 2020. https://www.leadershipiq.com/blogs/leadershipiq/35354241-why-new-hires-fail-emotional-intelligence-vs-skills

Chapter 6: Find your confidence

1. MacIntyre, Peter D., et al. 'Conceptualizing Willingness to Communicate in a L2: A Situational Model of L2 Confidence and Affiliation.' *The Modern Language Journal*, vol. 82, no. 4, 1998.
2. Monarth, Harrison and Larina Kase. *The Confident Speaker*, New York: McGraw-Hill, 2007. If you suffer from speaking anxiety, I highly recommend this book. The authors discuss speaking anxiety in detail and refer to the 'four horsemen of anxiety' as 'biology, mood, behaviour and thinking'. It also includes a short anxiety assessment to determine how severe these responses are for you.

3. Charlotte Lieberman, 'Why You Procrastinate (It Has Nothing to Do With Self-Control)' *New York Times*, 25 March 2019. https://www.nytimes.com/2019/03/25/smarter-living/why-you-procrastinate-it-has-nothing-to-do-with-self-control.html

Chapter 7: Body language from a box

1. Microsoft, '2021 Work Trend Index Annual Report: The Next Great Disruption is Hybrid Work. Are We Ready?' 22 March 2021. This report is available for download here: https://www.microsoft.com/en-us/worklab/work-trend-index/hybrid-work
2. Hessels, Roy S. 'How Does Gaze to Faces Support Face-to-Face Interaction? A Review and Perspective', *Psychonomic Bulletin and Review*, 27(5), pp. 856–81. New York: Springer, October 2020.
3. Moyers, Bill. *A World of Ideas*. New York: Doubleday, 1989.

Chapter 8: A voice that flows like honey

1. Kraus, M. W. 'Voice-only Communication Enhances Empathic Accuracy', *American Psychologist*, 72(7), pp. 644–54. American Psychological Association, 2017.
2. Karpf, Anne. *The Human Voice: The Story of a Remarkable Talent*. London: Bloomsbury, 2011.
3. Carreyrou, John. *Bad Blood: Secrets and Lies in a Silicon-Valley Startup*. Picador, 2018.
4. Newman, Eryn and Norbert Schwarz. 'Good Sound, Good Research: How Audio Quality Influences Perceptions of the Research and Researcher', *Science Communication*, 40, 246–57. American Psychological Association, 2018.

Chapter 9: Bad English – good for business

1. This comment was made by one of my clients in our first consultation in 2010. At the time he was Vice President, Greater Asia for an American multinational company and was based in Singapore.
2. Heather Hansen, '2 Billion Voices: How to Speak Bad English Perfectly' TEDx Odense 2018. This talk can be viewed online here: https://www.ted.com/talks/heather_hansen_2_billion_voices_how_to_speak_bad_english_perfectly
3. Crystal, David. 'Two Thousand Million?', *English Today*, 24(1), pp. 36. Cambridge: Cambridge University Press, 2008.
4. According to linguist Braj Kachru's definition of inner circle English speakers: Kachru, B. (1985). Standards, codification and sociolinguistic realism: English language in the outer circle. In R. Quirk and H. Widowson (Eds.), *English in the world: Teaching and learning the language and literatures* (p. 11–36). Cambridge: Cambridge University Press.
5. Lennox Morrison, 'Native Speakers are the World's Worst Communicators', BBC Workplace online article: https://www.bbc.com/worklife/article/20161028-native-english-speakers-are-the-worlds-worst-communicators, 31 October 2016.
6. Härén, Fredrik. *One World One Company*, p. 18. Interesting Books, 2013.

Chapter 10: Understand and be understood

1. You can learn more about the Plain English Campaign here: http://www.plainenglish.co.uk/
2. You can find the Plain English Campaign's Crystal Mark Standards here: http://www.plainenglish.co.uk/services/crystal-mark/frequently-asked-questions.html
3. A 50th Anniversary edition of this book is publicly available: https://docs.voanews.eu/en-US-LEARN/2014/02/15/7f8de955-596b-437c-ba40-a68ed754c348.pdf

4. Nerrière, Jean-Paul and David Hon. *Globish the World Over*, (ebook). International Globish Institute, 2009.
5. James Emil Flege, 'Detection of French accent by native English speakers', *The Journal of the Acoustical Society of America* 73, S30-S30 (1983).
6. Huang, L., Frideger, M., & Pearce, J. L. (2013, August 12). 'Political Skill: Explaining the Effects of Nonnative Accent on Managerial Hiring and Entrepreneurial Investment Decisions'. *Journal of Applied Psychology*. Advance online publication
7. Timming, A.R. 'The effect of foreign accent on employability: a study of the aural dimensions of aesthetic labour in customer-facing and non-customer-facing jobs'. *Work, Employment and Society*. 2017;31(3):409–28.
8. Read the full story in Chapter 5.
9. Hockett, Charles F. *A Course in Modern Linguistics*. New York: Macmillan, 1958.
10. Jenner, B. 1989. 'Teaching Pronunciation: The Common Core', *Speak Out!* (21), pp. 10–14.
11. Jenkins, Jennifer. *The Phonology of English as an International Language*, p. 126 Oxford: Oxford University Press, 2000.
12. Robin Walker wrote a more accessible guide for language practitioners in 2010, *Teaching the Pronunciation of English as a Lingua Franca*, which showed how teachers could integrate the LFC into the language classroom.

Chapter 11: The key to happiness

1. This quote comes from Robert Waldinger's November 2015 TEDx Beacon Street Talk: 'What Makes a Good Life? Lessons from the Longest Study on Happiness'. https://www .ted.com/talks/robert_waldinger_what_makes_a_good_life_lessons_from_the_longest _study_on_happiness
2. Holt-Lunstad, J., Smith, T. B., Layton, J.B. (2010) 'Social Relationships and Mortality Risk: A Meta-analytic Review'. *PloS Med* 7(7)
3. The Institute of Leadership and Management published the results of their January 2020 survey in a report titled 'New Decade, New Directions'. The full report can be downloaded from their website: https://www.institutelm.com/resourceLibrary/new-decade-new-direction.html
4. King, Marisa. *Social Chemistry: Decoding the Patterns of Human Connection.*
5. Microsoft, '2021 Work Trend Index Annual Report: The Next Great Disruption is Hybrid Work. Are We Ready?' 22 March 2021. This report is available for download here: https:/ /www.microsoft.com/en-us/worklab/work-trend-index/hybrid-work
6. Jeppe Vilstrup, CEO of Innovisor. Interview with the author, April 20, 2021.
7. Nummenmaa, Lauri, and Enrico Glerean, Riitta Hari, Jari K. Hietanen. 'Bodily Map of Emotions', *Proceedings of the National Academy of Sciences*, 111(2), pp. 646–51. Washington DC: National Academy of Sciences, January 2014.
8. Goleman, Daniel. *Emotional Intelligence: Why It Can Matter More Than IQ*. London: Bloomsbury, 2020.
9. The Edelman Trust Barometer has been published every year since 2001 and is typically released in March. You can download the full report and analysis on their website: www.edelman.com
10. Scott, Kim. *Radical Candor: How to Get What You Want by Saying What You Mean*. Pan MacMillan, 2019.
11. Microsoft '2021 World Trend Index Annual Report: The Next Great Disruption is Hybrid Work – Are We Ready for It?' Available for download here: https://www.microsoft.com/ en-us/worklab/work-trend-index/hybrid-work
12. Hall, J., N. Pennington, and A. Holmstrom. 'Connecting through Technology during COVID-19', *Human Communication & Technology*, 2(1). 2021.
13. Ibid.
14. Kraus, M. W. 'Voice-only Communication Enhances Empathic Accuracy', *American Psychologist*, 72(7), pp. 644–54. 2017.

Chapter 12: We're all connected (or not)

1. A question posed by a global Head of HR during a public webinar I delivered titled 'Connected Leadership'. 17 February 2021.
2. Tichy, N., M. Tushman, and C. Fombrun. 'Social Network Analysis for Organizations', *The Academy of Management Review*, 4(4), pp. 507–19. 1979.
3. Corritore, Matthew, Amir Goldberg, and Sameer B. Srivastava. 'The New Analytics of Culture', *Harvard Business Review*, 98(1), pp. 77–83. 2020.
4. Henry Ward explains his reasoning for conducting organizational network analysis in this blog post from 12 September 2017: https://carta.com/blog/the-shadow-organizatio nal-chart/#
5. Lalleman, Richard Santos. 'How to Rethink Change with the Three Percent Rule', Academy to Innovate HR (AIHR), https://www.aihr.com/blog/rethink-change-three-percent-rule/
6. Interview with the author, 20 April 2021.
7. Ibid.
8. Leonardi, Paul, and Noshir Contractor. 'Better People Analytics', *Harvard Business Review*, 96(6), pp. 70–81. 2018.
9. 2018 Deloitte Global Human Capital Trends, 'People Data: How Far Is Too Far?'. https://www2.deloitte.com/ph/en/pages/human-capital/articles/global-human-capital-trends-2 018.html

Chapter 13: Creating a safe environment

1. Ethington, Philip J. 'The Intellectual Construction of "Social Distance": Toward a Recovery of Georg Simmel's Social Geometry', *Cybergeo: European Journal of Geography*, 16 September 1997. http://journals.openedition.org/cybergeo/227
2. Microsoft, '2021 Work Trend Index Annual Report: The Next Great Disruption is Hybrid Work. Are We Ready?' 22 March 2021. This report is available for download here: https://www.microsoft.com/en-us/worklab/work-trend-index/ hybrid-work
3. Neeley, Tsedal. 'Organizational Behavior Reading: Leading Global Teams', *Harvard Business School Core Curriculum Readings Series*. Boston: Harvard Business Publishing, 30 June 2018. See also: Neeley, Tsedal. 'Global Teams That Work', *Harvard Business Review*, pp. 74–81. October 2015. Neeley, Tsedal. *Remote Work Revolution: Succeeding from Anywhere*. New York: Harper Business, 2021.
4. Neeley spent several years following the 'Englishnization' of Rakuten, the largest online retailer in Japan. Her very interesting findings are documented in her book: *The Language of Global Success: How a Common Tongue Transforms Multinational Organizations*. Princeton: Princeton University Press, 2017.
5. Aristotle, 'What Google Learned from Its Quest to Build the Perfect Team', *New York Times* Magazine, 28 February 2016. https://www.nytimes.com/2016/02/28/magazine/ what-google-learned-from-its-quest-to-build-the-perfect-team.html
6. Edmondson, A. 'Psychological Safety and Learning Behavior in Work Teams', *Administrative Science Quarterly*, 44(2), pp. 350–83. 1999.
7. Learn more about the different factors Google studied in their guide to Project Aristotle: https://rework.withgoogle.com/print/guides/5721312655835136/
8. Sara Blakely has told this story in multiple interviews that are freely available online. I took this quote from a short Business Insider clip that highlights just this story: https:// www.youtube.com/watch?v=OZEPbyIA8XI
9. Edmondson, Amy. *The Fearless Organization: Creating Psychological Safety in the Workplace for Learning, Innovation and Growth*. New York: Wiley, 2018.
10. Ibid. You can find these survey statements in Amy Edmondson's original 1999 research or her book.

Chapter 14: Human skills that build connection

1. Sophia made this statement at the 2018 Discovery Conference in Toronto, Canada as quoted by Editor Stephan Law in *Electronic Products and Technology* Magazine May 2018. P4 https://issuu.com/glaciermedia/docs/ept_mayjune2018_laz_de
2. Anita Williams Woolley, et al. 'Evidence for a Collective Intelligence Factor in the Performance of Human Groups', *Science* 330, pp 686–8, 2010. View online: http://www.cs.cmu.edu/~ab/Salon/research/Woolley_et_al_Science_2010-2.pdf
3. Neeley, Tsedal. 'Global Teams That Work', *Harvard Business Review*, pp. 74–81. October 2015.

Chapter 15: Connecting online – the new netiquette

1. Microsoft '2021 World Trend Index Annual Report: The Next Great Disruption is Hybrid Work – Are We Ready for It?' Available for download here: https://www.microsoft.com/en-us/worklab/work-trend-index/hybrid-work
2. Chuq Von Rospach, 'A Primer on How to Work With the USENET Community', 4 June 1984, https://www.krsaborio.net/internet/research/1984/0603.htm
3. Email correspondence with the author 24–26 March 2021.
4. Chuq Von Rospach, 'A Primer on How to Work With the USENET Community', 4 June 1984, https://www.krsaborio.net/internet/research/1984/0603.htm
5. Shea, Virginia. *Netiquette*. San Francisco: Albion Books, 1994. http://www.albion.com/netiquette/book/index.html
6. Taylor, Shirley. *E-Mail Etiquette*. London: Marshall Cavendish, 2010. This book's popularity led to an updated edition in 2017, now titled *Email Essentials*.
7. Jared Spataro, '2 Years of Digital Transformation in 2 Months', Microsoft 365 Blog, April 30, 2020. https://www.microsoft.com/en-us/microsoft-365/blog/2020/04/30/2-years-digital-transformation-2-months/

Chapter 16: Unmuting yourself

1. Learn more about the Global DISC assessment at www.icq.global
2. Yoodli is an AI-enabled public speaking application that can help you identify and quantify your public speaking progress. Learn more at www.yoodli.ai

Chapter 17: Unmuting your organization

1. Learn more about the Failure Institute's Fuckup Nights events here: www.fuckupnights.com

🎙 Acknowledgements

Without the support and encouragement of many important people in my life, I'm not sure I would have had the courage to unmute myself and write this book.

Thank you to my long-time friend, Shirley Taylor, for pushing me out of my comfort zone (yet again) and reminding me to play bigger. Her multiple rounds of feedback on the first manuscript absolutely made this book a better read.

Thank you to my agent, Chris Newson, for believing in my ideas. This would have (quite literally) become a very different book without your involvement.

I am forever indebted to the amazing team at Bloomsbury: Matt James, my commissioning editor, for taking on this project, giving exceptional feedback and making insightful comments; and Allie Collins and her team of talented editors, fact-checkers, proofreaders and indexers. You all made the whole writing process seamless and fun. Of course, I take full responsibility for any oversights that might remain.

My clients and their stories are at the heart of this book. They have taught me so much and I'm grateful to them for inspiring me every day. I can't thank you enough for your support of my work, the lessons you've shared with me and our ongoing friendships. This book is for you.

My sincere admiration and gratitude goes to the many researchers, authors and leaders who are mentioned throughout this book and listed in the endnotes. Our world wouldn't be the same without your hard work. Thank you for inspiring me.

My global network of friends and colleagues, near and far, have always been available to offer a listening ear, read a chapter, or answer questions. You have all been instrumental in the success of this book. Special thanks to my parents and extended family along with my innermost circle of friends for your constant support, encouragement and champagne celebrations of every milestone.

Above all, thank you to my husband, Peter, and daughters, Victoria and Stella. Your love, understanding and support has been immense as you gave me the space and time to unmute.

🎤 About the Author

Heather Hansen is the founder and lead consultant for Singapore-based communication consultancy and training firm, Global Speech Academy Pte Ltd. She is also an External Expert in Communication for National University of Singapore (NUS) Business School's Executive Education programmes.

Heather helps leaders of diverse and dispersed teams build unmuted communication cultures that increase efficiency, innovation, inclusion and collaboration. She is also an outspoken advocate for global voices and linguistic inclusion as demonstrated by her popular 2018 TEDx talk titled *2 Billion Voices: How to speak bad English perfectly*.

Learn more about Heather's books and talks at www.heatherhansen.com.

🎙 Index